Pra

Betting

What a beautiful book. This is an unflinching, profoundly intimate account of a family at the forefront of organic food and community supported agriculture in California: heartbreaking, funny, honest, and above all, full of a deep and lasting respect for the earth.

—ALICE WATERS, OWNER OF CHEZ PANISSE

This is a gripping true story of how one family turned a patch of star thistle in California's Capay Valley into a thriving organic farm, starting in the 1970s. They were true pioneers and worked very hard, parents and children both, to get this farm off the ground. In the year 2000 the mother dies of cancer. The father drifts off, leaving the whole job up to the four sons. They couldn't have done it without the help of hardworking, reliable Mexican farm workers. Thaddeus tells the story with plenty of rich, informative detail. There are no wasted words. He learned how to farm the hard way and describes it all with vivid richness.

—R. CRUMB, AMERICAN CARTOONIST

This book captures life as a kid in the Capay Valley, where I grew up not far from the author, but what felt like a world away, on an Indian reservation the book mentions—once called Rumsey Indian Rancheria, and today known as the Yocha Dehe Wintun Nation. My cousins and I knew Thaddeus through school, and he always treated us with respect, but we were Native American and, as he acknowledges, our tribe faced struggles with the local community at the time. Little did I know, until reading this book, that our families shared so much in common. We all worked hard. We farmed. We fished, swam, and played in the same creek. Our mothers both knew backbreaking work in tomato fields in the searing Capay Valley heat. We also all knew loss and poverty. As *Betting on the Farm* shows, the Barsotti family and the Yocha Dehe people today share the same values and vision—a commitment to feeding people, growing sustainable food, and protecting this magnificent Capay Valley that is our home.

—JAMES KINTER, TRIBAL COUNCIL SECRETARY AND
PROPERTY FARM & RANCH CHAIRMAN, YOCHA DEHE WINTUN NATION

In *Betting on the Farm*, Thaddeus Barsotti captures the grit it took to grow up in a loving but broken and poor family, whose parents went back to the land to become first-generation farmers. Barsotti pulls no punches as he and his brothers face the arduous tasks of learning from the land and those who worked it, agricultural practices that made him one of America's leaders in sustainable agriculture. Heart-wrenching and visceral, it's a tale I couldn't put down.

—ANN M. EVANS, FORMER MAYOR, DAVIS, CALIFORNIA,
AUTHOR OF AWARD-WINNING *THE DAVIS FARMERS MARKET COOKBOOK*

Betting on the Farm provides a great appreciation for a family committed to feeding people. Thad effortlessly captures the grit and emotion of his family's perseverance through loss, and the broader story of the struggles of a family farm, that was very forward-thinking for its time. The words make the story come to life off the page and easily take me back to the fields and to my time as a farmworker. This is the story many do not see when they sit at a Michelin-starred restaurant or purchase their organic produce at a local market.

—ERIC GUERRA, SACRAMENTO CITY MAYOR PRO TEM

Lots of tears from me in the first chapter. A very emotional story for me to read, but I stayed up until five thirty in the morning finishing it! I felt a little beat up at the end, but it was fair. I regret being so distant during those times. I love all my boys and am very proud of them. This story does not talk much about their amazing success. Kathy would not believe it; it is hard for me to believe.

—MARTIN BARNES, FATHER OF THADDEUS BARSOTTI

BETTING ON THE FARM

Thaddeus Barsotti

BETTING ON THE FARM

AN HEIRLOOM CHILDHOOD

FARM MEMOIR

U.S. Nº1

GROWN IN CAPAY
CALIFORNIA

BY
THADDEUS BARSOTTI

THE FOUNDING OF AMERICA'S LARGEST
COMMUNITY SUPPORTED
AGRICULTURE PROGRAM, FARM FRESH
TO YOU, AND THE HARD-WON
TRANSITION OF AN ORGANIC FAMILY
FARM TO ITS SECOND GENERATION

WATERSIDE PRODUCTIONS
CARDIFF-BY-THE-SEA

ISBN-13: 978-1-960583-45-1 print edition
ISBN-13: 978-1-960583-46-8 e-book edition

Waterside Productions
2055 Oxford Ave
Cardiff, CA 92007
www.waterside.com

This is dedicated to my mom.
If only you could see us now!
Miss you.

Acknowledgments

Getting a book into a finished format takes a lot more than just writing down the story. At the beginning of this journey, I had no idea of the many different folks who would be needed to support the creation of this. Arriving at the end of the journey, I can look back over the process and be grateful for the folks who helped make this happen.

Thanks to:

My wife Moyra for always being there with full support, practical feedback and gentle nudges to get this done.

My brothers Noah and Freeman for supporting me to tell this story, which belongs to them as much as it belongs to me.

My late brother Che, who once told me that when he got over Mom dying he was going to write that story down. Well, here it is Che. Wish you could read it and let me know what you think.

Farm Fresh To You customers. For my entire life you all have been there to support our farm and family. Your support has been relied upon and used more than you all will ever know.

Ruby Peru for help in making the manuscript as easy and entertaining to read as it is.

Josh Freel for proofreading in accordance with the rules and preferences of *Merriam-Webster's Unabridged Dictionary* and the *Chicago Manual of Style*, 17th edition.

Philip Harris for designing the cover art, Wesley Coker for creating the chapter illustrations, and Christy Salinas for the book design.

Waterside Productions for facilitating the publication of this book and making some very important introductions.

Table of Contents

Chapter One

Below one of the Capay Valley's signature pink sunsets, heirloom tomatoes a week away from harvest hung heavy on the vine. A hospice nurse drove her dusty old Ford down our gravel driveway, past the Capay Fruits & Vegetables sign. An oncologist had already explained to me how Mom's lungs were now less efficient at transferring oxygen to her red blood cells, which was why she had to gulp down air just to breathe. So, when Mom's breathing turned into gasping like someone emerging from underwater, we finally called Yolo Hospice and they sent the nurse.

Inside the house, she stood before us, almost formally, hands clasped in front of a neat, button-down shirt embroidered with the hospice logo. Mom's husband Terry, her parents, her sister Dianna, and I gathered while the nurse's question pierced the warm, dense fog of denial that had, so far, kept the five of us sane.

"Oncologists treat cancer, but when you accept hospice care, that means you accept that you're no longer treating the disease," the nurse said. Summer sweat cemented a strand of hair to her forehead as she continued. "Hospice care focuses on making the end as comfortable as possible. Kathleen Barsotti, do you accept hospice care?"

The nurse waited patiently for an answer—eyes averted, face devoid of emotion. She had her directive. She could not help my mother until the patient faced the fact of her own imminent demise.

Hysterical sobs welled up inside me. The effort to push them down felt like lifting dumbbells with my throat. A painful constriction engulfed my head until I trembled, and no sooner did I calm myself than another wave of hysteria crashed upon me. I struggled again to stay steady, though, for Mom.

To answer no would have relegated my mother to more chemo, but doctors had already said her bones were "swiss cheese" for lack of a more medical term, and her white blood cell count was too low for more chemo. Since she stopped the treatments, we had witnessed her lesions and cracked lips healing, although her hair, eyebrows, and eyelashes had not grown back. Absent the side-effect-inducing chemo, Mom appeared to be getting better, which gave us false hope that she had more time. But, of course, even though we could not directly see the cancer proliferating, unchecked, on its final spree through her body, my mother, aged fifty-one, was definitely dying.

None of us really understood how all our lives would change when Mom said yes to the hospice nurse. We only knew that doctors and western medicine could do nothing more for her. The nurse, though, had been through scenes like this many times before. We took heart in the nurse's confidence and understood she was equipped to walk not just Mom, but all of us, to The End.

"Yes," my mother whispered. "I accept hospice care."

For us, the nurse brought little, blue books that described what to expect through this process. The grief, anger, and frustration were all detailed in paragraph form, with handy timelines. On the back of the books, an illustration of a sailboat floating off into the horizon was accompanied by a quote: *Just as they leave this world, they are arriving in another.*

The nurse wheeled an oxygen machine into the house and showed us how to use it. I would soon be surprised by how quickly my mother grew dependent upon this machine to breathe. The others left the room to go sob in private while the nurse looked for a place in the fridge to stash Mom's morphine, which would help manage the pain. The oxygen machine hummed as my mother sat up with great effort and adjusted the cannula under her nose.

When we were finally alone, Mom broke down and wept.

I said, "That wasn't very fun, was it?"

She sobbed a big, wet, "No."

Mom's difficulty breathing soon forced her to stop crying, though, and she joked that she might as well buck up, as crying used too much oxygen.

The first of Mom's four sons to arrive home that July, I had turned twenty years old just two weeks before. She laughed when she first saw me, all skinny with a spindly beard from having spent the last few months in Mexico. In order to learn to communicate with the farm workers, I had enrolled in a Spanish language school in Guanajuato for my spring quarter. The plan was for me to return that summer to help Mom harvest twenty full acres of heirloom tomatoes—the most she had ever planted. It never occurred to me I would be galivanting around Mexico during Mom's last few months of life.

My arrival was soon followed by that of Che, one of my twin eldest brothers, on vacation from the Coast Guard. Che's visit, rather than Mom's looming death, which none of us expected, was originally the thing that had prompted the four brothers to gather at home that week.

After Che, his twin Noah, a commodities broker in San Francisco, pulled up in his beat-up, old, red Chevy Beretta. The paint on the top of this car had oxidized completely, except for one small spot that for some reason looked perfect. On that spot, Noah had affixed a yellow "Mystery Spot, Santa Cruz, CA," bumper sticker. This car was proof that making money in the city could be just as hard as it was on this farm.

I remember seeing our youngest brother Freeman, aged sixteen, for the first time in a long time when he pulled up in the driveway. When he saw my face, his expression changed, and I realized I must have worn a stricken look that told him, *everything's different now.* Freeman was returning from attending a program called Boys' State, put on by the American Legion, where he had been making new friends and learning all about state government.

To him, Mom looked about the same as when he had left, but he could see in my eyes that, to me, she looked much worse than the last time I saw her, months ago. As the only brother still living at home, perhaps Freeman should have seen the end coming, but he didn't. This wasn't his fault. For him, being with Mom every day, as she steadily withered away, made it harder to see how close she was gradually coming to death. After all, over the past five years of her cancer relapse, Mom's hair fell out from the chemo, but she kept running the farm. A brain tumor made her blind in one eye, but she kept running the farm. A vertebra in her spine spontaneously shattered, but she kept running the farm.

Che and Noah—twenty-five-year-olds pursuing new careers, romances, and ambitions—had not put their lives on pause due to the cancer either. We were all used to Mom managing the farm full time with her breast cancer. We thought it could go on like that forever.

At the time, I thought Mom did not know she was going to die until that moment with the hospice nurse, but, in retrospect, I now realize she had already hired a farm manager for the first time: her own replacement, scheduled to start at the end of the summer. He was a fraternity brother of Noah's from UC Davis. We all knew she had done this, but none of the brothers stopped and said, *Wait, that's weird.*

She knew.

In fact, it could not have been a coincidence that she died when Che just happened to be on leave from the Coast Guard, when Noah and I planned to come home to see him, and when Freeman returned from summer camp. Seldom, in those days, did all the brothers assemble at once. The truth of the matter is, our mother willfully delayed death until her boys were home, in the farmhouse.

In this house, in California's rural, western Yolo County, Mom had raised us among the dual fragrances of sweet pea blossoms and chicken manure. Sure, the fertile Capay Valley's promise had worn thin through a childhood spent duct-taping our shoes together and scrounging through cupboards filled with nothing but all-natural (but not fun to eat) food from the local co-op. Still, Mom had loved this land, our fucked-up little farm, and us, fiercely.

When my brothers arrived, we gathered around Mom's bedside, and I told everyone about the hospice nurse and the come-to-Jesus moment she had forced upon us.

Mom raised one of her non-eyebrows, smiled a little, and said, "I'd like to put that lady in a hole with a can of tuna."

It was a joke about how, as kids, we were tasked with eradicating the farm's population of feral cats that bred incessantly, overrunning the farm while pissing and defecating in every room of every building. The best method at that time was to dig a hole and place a can of tuna in the bottom of it. The starving creatures would overcome their fear of us to dash into the hole and eat the tuna. As they feasted, we shot them in the head with a .22 caliber rifle, then filled up the hole with dirt. Our farm was not some fairy-tale paradise, far from it, but it had always been real . . . maybe too real.

Our gentle mother did not actually want to shoot and bury the hospice nurse, of course. She only meant that while the hospice nurse—an angel who brought Mom oxygen and pain relief—was an innocent kitten, the deadly fact she forced us to confront was a mangy, feral cat. If only there were a hole somewhere into which we could lure Mom's cancer and shoot it dead.

That night, I felt that the opportunity to communicate with my mother in a lucid state was dwindling. The pain, morphine, and inevitable end were taking their toll. My heart gushed with love, my soul cried with sadness, but my brain chose words that metered the emotions fairly.

Mom looked at me with a confidence and knowledge of things about which I had no idea. "Thad," she said, "you have your whole life in front of you. You haven't even fallen in love, yet. That's fun!"

The day before that hospice nurse showed up, I remember being on the phone with some guy from our third-party organic certifying agency, CCOF (California Certified Organic Farmers). Plump heirloom tomatoes, our cash crop (to the extent that we had one then), already hung from sticky, pungent vines. Through the kitchen window, I could see the dense rows, polka-dotted with red, yellow, and purple fruit, just begging for harvest. Next to the tomatoes, tiny plantings of niche herbs, eggplant, peppers, cherry tomatoes, cucumbers, and okra, all just about ready to harvest, colored the farm like a mosaic. Meanwhile, a bureaucrat on the phone threatened to revoke our organic farm certification, treating one tiny piece of incomplete paperwork as if it were a personal issue for him. I found the threat incomprehensible, considering the fact that this farm had always been organic. We had never known any other way of farming. In fact, Mom and Dad pioneered chemical-free farming in this valley long before "organic certification" even existed. The idea that we (of all people!) were not farming in a certified organic manner was laughable.

I remember how, while I spoke to the man from CCOF, Mom, at the kitchen table—blind in one eye, skin covered in sores, stubble sticking out of her bald head like a baby chick—stared down a bowl of clam chowder like she was going to war with it.

I hung up the phone and asked her, "How long has this paperwork been due? Are we going to lose our certification?"

Mom shrugged.

"Isn't this a big deal?" I pressed.

She laughed a little. "Thaddeus," she said, filling a spoon with chowder, "when you're dying, nothing's all that important."

Until the hospice nurse showed up the next day, that was the most direct conversation we'd ever had about her death.

I remember how, later that day, Mom declared herself a champ for finishing the whole bowl of clam chowder, an accomplishment that seemed more important to her in the summer of 2000 than the twenty acres bulging with ripe tomatoes whose harvest would pay the farm's bills for the year . . . or not.

Mom's parents, "Grandma and Grandpa On-The-Hill"—who lived across the street on the first rise of the foothills that overlooked the Capay Valley—helped out full time at the end. During those last few weeks, our Aunt Dianna visited the farm daily too. Our stepfather Terry tried to be present for Mom, too, but his people skills were somewhat lacking. With so many cooks spoiling the broth, our mother's dying moments were not exactly full of Hallmark-card-worthy togetherness snapshots. In fact, as Mom gradually lost the ability to captain our ship, I saw how much worse our family's ill-equipped, seat-of-the-pants, back-to-nature lifestyle could get.

My stepfather Terry owned a farm of his own and had never lived with us. Over the years, though, he taught me a lot in the field about machines, farming practices, and crop management. We were friends of a sort, Terry and I. He was a father figure to me, but I may have been the only brother who felt that way.

I recall how, in the midst of the madness, Terry and his beagle Max entered the crowded family room where Mom lay on the couch. Oblivious to our human reality, Max excitedly greeted everyone, then proceeded to sit on one of Mom's oxygen tubes that snaked around the room.

Aunt Dianna, at the end of her rope, yelled, "Get that dog out of here!" as if Terry was something less than a full-fledged member of the family, something less than Mom's husband.

With a pointed finger, Terry responded, "Don't you raise your voice to me!"

Dianna snapped back, the dog yelped, and then somebody kicked everyone out of the house. I think that was actually Freeman. He was not your typical sixteen-year-old. None of us had been.

The stress was too much. Terry did not return after that.

Somewhere in all this madness, Grandma disowned my brother Noah. She had done this a few times, actually. In retrospect, each time we visited, she used to tell us the same World War II stories and show us her same favorite flower. She may have been declining into dementia even as her daughter died of cancer.

Aunt Dianna warned us brothers, "It's time to have barf bowls handy. Your mom won't want to eat, but we have to force her to!"

Our aunt courted madness in her own way. I mean, who forces a dying woman to eat? Everybody wanted to control something in those final days, so we hassled each other over inconsequential decisions and imagined emergencies that felt important at the time. Surely, anyone describing death as "peaceful" or "restful" never met the Barsotti/ Barnes family.

In the midst of this hellscape, but still a couple of weeks before my brothers arrived and the incident with the dog, our stepfather Terry showed a dark side of himself. Standing on the front porch, thumbs hooked behind suspenders, mustache quivering on his upper lip, Terry overlooked the farm and commented with a fake laugh, "Someday, this will all be mine."

This was enough to get the gears in my mother's head turning. If asked, Terry would have said his statement was a joke, and maybe he even thought it was, but this telling moment was yet another little detail that, to Mom, put her husband under suspicion. Terry had been a good husband, a good farmer, and a stable stepfather in his own way, but he was controlling and inflexible when it came to money. Mom loved him, but at the end of the day, the five of us—we four boys and Mom—were "the family." Terry stood on the periphery of our family, as did our biological father.

Mom wanted us boys alone to control the farm after she passed, and not for Terry to add her twenty acres to his own holdings. At the same time, Mom felt conflicted about wanting at least one of us to take over this project to which she had dedicated her life. I realized this one day in the kitchen, when, as Mom dealt with money issues (yet again) she confessed to me, "Thad, I don't know if I'm doing you a favor by encouraging you to get involved in farming."

Mom never sugarcoated the toil of it all, the stress, the never-ending unpredictability and unprecedented challenges, nor did she hide her absolute love for this land. It was no secret, though, that she wanted us to keep the farm. In her will, she had originally made Terry the farm's trustee, but that was supposed to make things easier for us, not harder. So, just a few weeks before her death, when Mom had heard enough of Terry's subtle comments about how he planned to take over the farm, she knew he could no longer be the trustee. She picked up the phone and made an appointment with her attorney. That decision to make us responsible for the farm right away changed everything for us boys. It not only affected the rest of that summer, but it changed our lives, forever.

I remember the searing summer day when I wheeled Mom out to my silver Ford Ranger and helped her into it. I had to rent a wheelchair to get Mom, on her spindly legs, even ten steps outside the house, but even with that reality right in my face, I still did not realize this would be her last trip out of the house, her last drive down the road, her last view of the Capay countryside. So many lasts.

We drove past her newly planted two-acre Meyer lemon grove—Mom's most recent initiative, which she had not even seen yet. She smiled with pleasure as we passed and said the trees would yield a good crop in a few years. I realize now that when Mom had it planted, she already knew she would never see a single one of those lemons.

While I drove, Mom mused, "I never thought this day would come."

I wasn't sure if she meant the day she stopped trusting Terry or the day she realized she was really going to die. Maybe she meant the day she had to race to an attorney's office against the ticking clock of her own death. I will never know.

After signing the documents in the attorney's office in Sacramento, Mom abruptly declared, "We have to leave NOW." I suspected what was coming.

Fast walking, I pushed her wheelchair down the hall, hoping to ditch the attorney, but he followed, making friendly small talk. Meanwhile, Mom emptied the contents of her purse into her lap.

Just as we reached the elevator, she puked, quite violently yet neatly, into the purse. The attorney took it in stride. As the elevator door closed, Mom looked up and said goodbye to the attorney with a meek smile, and he waved back. The vomiting resumed in the elevator, all the way down to the ground floor, through the building's doors, and down the sidewalk.

People could not help but stare as we passed. I wanted to tell the goggle-eyed people around us: *The woman puking before you is a trail-blazer of the organic foods movement. The woman puking before you is the most loving soul on earth, and I'm proud to be the person pushing this chair.*

On the forty-five-minute drive home, we rode mostly in silence. I still thought I would have plenty of time for talking, the rest of the summer at least, otherwise I would have told her about my adventures in Mexico, asked about her plans for the lemon orchard, pressed her for answers to the moral quandaries life brings every day, and simply experienced the unique, loving connection we shared. Instead, I just drove.

I remember how when we stopped at the stop sign in the town of Madison, she said, "The one thing I wish I did more with you boys was go camping more often."

I did not realize these were the last regrets of a dying woman, and to my own eternal regret, I didn't even reply.

Arriving home, I wheeled Mom back into the house. It had been a big day for her, and her exhaustion was met with sleep. For me, knowing the responsibility of the farm had now been clearly passed on to my brothers and me changed my focus. Instead of dwelling on what had happened at the attorney's office, I immediately occupied my mind and soul with the work of the farm. There were fields to check, broken pieces of equipment to fix, field crews to direct, crops to sell, supplies to order, and, most importantly, relationships with key produce buyers to nurture. Managing the office and the bills would be entirely new challenges for me, but who else was going to deal with that?

The night it happened, I slept on a couch in the room where I was born, where Mom lay in bed. A summer breeze through an open window riffled the curtains. Freeman slept on the rug below me. Che and Noah joined Grandma and Grandpa standing vigil by the bedside.

I awoke to Grandma saying, "That's it. She's gone."

I jostled Freeman to wake him.

Che, with one hand on Mom's pulse, looked at his watch. He said, "No, not yet." A moment later, he said, "Now she's gone. 1:10 a.m."

It was July 2, 2000. The oxygen machine registered a total of 185.9 hours of use.

Grandpa collapsed and sobbed like a baby, and I suddenly realized I had been so wrapped up in the fact that I was losing my mother that I never really considered his point of view. That poor man was losing his little girl.

While we waited for hospice to show up, Grandma made tea. I remember how Grandpa gestured his cup of tea toward Mom's lifeless corpse, saying, "No tea for you, Kathy." We all chuckled at that—our way of acknowledging a mutually felt relief that her death was finally over. The last few days waiting for the inevitable had been hell. Now, at least, we could move on to whatever would be next.

When the hospice nurse arrived, I expected her to check on Mom immediately to ensure our assessment of "dead" was right, but there really was no confusion as to what had happened. Her body was no longer living. It was even starting to bloat.

Freeman had the foresight to remove the one piece of jewelry Mom was wearing: her wedding ring from Terry. It should have been easy. After all, the ring was sized for healthy Mom and had recently become too large for her spindly cancer fingers, but the bloating happened so quickly that the ring almost didn't come off. Watching my dear brother pry the ring off Mom's dead body made us all giggle for some reason. What was happening to us?

When she arrived, the nurse's first question caught me completely off guard, and it took my mind a few moments to even register the question: "Where's the morphine?"

Shocked, I walked her over to the refrigerator, instead of to our dead mother, and showed her the huge bottle that was in the door, next to the milk. She opened it and dumped it down the drain of the kitchen sink. In hindsight, it's a shame. That morphine might have come in handy over the next few months.

We stayed up all night, contemplating the first moments of this new world, this world without Mom. A second set of hospice folks arrived and rolled our mother out the door in a zipped-up body bag. We all stood on the front patio made of warm, adobe bricks, watching Mom make her last trip out of the farmhouse she had built, the house in which I was born, the house in which she died.

It was still dark, so it seemed strange that a mockingbird started singing just then. It sang a beautiful song as if to tell us everything would be okay. The four brothers stood still, silently watching men load Mom into a van and listening to that bird.

Che broke the silence, saying, "Mom used to say that when people die, their spirits come back as birds."

We all believed that the bird, singing in the dark, was in fact our mother, or at least her spirit. Che would later refer to the presence of that bird as one of the few miracles he had witnessed in his life.

On the evening before Mom's funeral, a week or so after her death, the hogbacks of the hills surrounding her farm gleamed golden with dry grass. Cartoonish puffy clouds cast afternoon shadows across this familiar summertime terrain. By then, Grandma had disowned all of us. Furthermore, she insisted we refrain from telling our father, Martin Barnes, and his entire side of the family, about Mom's death. It was not just that they weren't invited to the funeral; Grandma didn't even think they deserved to know Mom had passed.

Dad's father, two brothers, and one brother-in-law all boast PhDs and careers in academia. Dad chose not to be bound by academia and pursued his countercultural life in defiance of such institutions. I don't know what his family really thought of that decision, but there were phases of tension and support, each ebbing and flowing through the different chapters of our parents' lives. When Mom and Dad were first married, Mom had been duly impressed by the Barnes family members, with their class, intellect, and family pride. In the beginning, she was embraced as a member of their family. Her intellectual capacity and beauty were easy to see. But, as one would expect, that embrace also ebbed and flowed over the course of my parents' rocky marriage. After the divorce, each family took sides with its own blood, leaving my brothers and me to wonder which blood flowed through our veins.

Despite their differences with Martin, the Barnes family would never acknowledge to Mom his issues with responsibility, his manipulative nature, and his dalliances with women—all of which lead to the divorce. Martin was excellent at reshaping the conversation, bringing in just the right amount of dirt at the right time to discredit Mom, painting a good enough picture of himself as the victim to make it easy for his family to take his side. In all honesty, why would they not? Due to the perception of my mother and her family that Dad's family eventually adopted, cold hard facts about Martin and his disruptive and damaging behavior fell on deaf ears. Meanwhile, my mother's side, the Barsotti family, shared a feeling that some members of the Barnes family had made my mother the scapegoat for Martin's troubles with life.

Grandma Barsotti's response to all this was to hold the entire Barnes family responsible for Mom's cancer. Because Martin and his shenanigans had, for years, been a constant source of stress for Mom, and because the Barneses had never held Martin responsible for his behavior—even condoning it at times—a decade-old rift had developed between the two families. Since the divorce, brewing resentments from the Barsottis had grown even stronger. Grandma Barsotti was so influential that most, if not all, of those close to Mom, including Mom, agreed with her about the cause of the cancer.

Mom's heartbeat had been the only thing that kept the expression of these negative emotions at bay, and with her death, the floodgates opened. With the benefit of hindsight, I now see that we all had in common a shared need to blame somebody for what went wrong with each of our families after my parents' divorce. The Barnes family blamed Mom for kicking Martin off the farm, causing him to flounder through the middle of his life. Our mother inexplicably died of cancer, which the Barsotti family believed to be caused by stress due to Martin's behavior, so they blamed Martin and whoever supported him. Blaming one another solved none of our problems, of course, but we didn't see that at the time.

In my opinion, the epic failure of my parents' relationship was clearly tied to a lack of understanding of where they each wanted their lives to end up. In their youth, amid swirling lust and shared ideological values, they never stopped to ask where they were headed, and, when the blissful season of that youth ended, what the next season would look like. When my parents were first married, had anyone asked my father where he wanted to be when he was fifty, he would have answered: doing the same thing he was doing at the time, which was fighting the machine, figuring the money out one week at a time, and remaining completely untethered. My mother's answer, on the other hand, would have included stability, a family, enough money to go on vacations, and a plan for retirement.

It's ironic that this mismatch was the "secret sauce" that created my existence. I also find irony in recognizing that my mother and her family blamed all her stress on Martin, not the fact that she was running a struggling small business in rural Yolo County. My father's family blamed my mother for stealing Martin's potential because they, in fact, were so patriarchal they could not comprehend the value that a woman brought to the success of Martin's business endeavors. Because of these many conflicts, my parents' progressive ideal of rethinking America's food system was intrinsically limited by certain narrow-minded, self-serving, cynical thought patterns. The combination caused my parents' relationship to fail epically, but not before they gave birth to the four of us and the company that we still run.

Gathering on the porch the evening after our mother died, we brothers passed around a basket of summer strawberries—the year's last harvest, super sweet from the July heat. The cool, tail end of a delta breeze provided relief from the summer sun. A little brown bird flitted here and there, chirping a song in a language I felt I ought to understand after spending my life on this farm.

Called a "flycatcher," this common songbird started its work for the day just as we relaxed from ours, often with the intoxicating scent of tomato vines on our clothes and skin. True to its name, the next time it flitted past, the bird held a bright blue dragonfly in its beak. Dinner was served.

Che smiled to see the fly catcher's victory and said, "I guess one of us should call Dad."

"Grandma said not to," I replied.

With furrowed brow, Noah asked, "You're serious?"

Freeman and I glanced at each other, and I realized teams were forming.

I wanted to do things as Grandma had asked, and Freeman seemed to also. We were loyal to the Barsotti clan and the memory of our mother who blamed Dad for her cancer.

Noah and Che—seven years older than me and nine years older than Freeman—understood this anger, but they, more than Freeman and me, remembered Martin as their father. He had been part of this family all the way up through most of their high school years. How could they not tell Dad about Mom?

In the garden, a cat had a field mouse in its mouth, but another cat wanted it too. I pointed out the drama, and we all watched as the black cat hunched up, ready to fight for its catch, and the tabby contemplated the risk of trying to steal the meal away. This struggle for dominance and survival had never failed to entertain us, and we monitored the contest until the challenger charged. The screeching sound of a cat fight pierced the air, then silence. The tabby emerged victorious, grabbing the mangled but still-alive mouse in its mouth and trotting off to enjoy its prize in private.

A moment later, much to Noah and Che's surprise, Freeman admitted he agreed with me about not telling Dad about Mom's death.

We all argued, which led to shouting and accusations of disloyalty. The scene got ugly.

Looking back, I see the silliness of my position. How could we not tell our father about his ex-wife's death? He would certainly find out soon enough, anyway, from others. I was so very angry, though. I wanted somebody to blame for losing Mom when she was only fifty-one. The idea of banding together as one big, loving family in the wake of this tragedy seemed impossible to me. Mom had told us boys to always stick together, no matter what, but everything felt fractured. I realized, too late, that Mom had been like a rope, single-handedly tying all of us, and the farm itself, together. Without her, the bonds were breaking at a rate of speed we never thought possible.

More flycatchers flitted past, collecting the innumerable insects that made July in Capay Valley a mixed blessing. I walked away from the scene with the excuse that I had to turn off some irrigation water and check on the evening's tomato packing, feeling lucky that the farm never failed to offer distractions from family drama. As I walked away, it crossed my mind that maybe it would be better to leave this place altogether and never come back. By the time the sun set in shades of orange and pink, none of the brothers wanted to see the others again. After the screen door slammed a final time on the dark, empty porch, the last of our strawberries spilled from their overturned basket and left a red stain on the earthen bricks.

Before going to bed, Noah and Che called Dad and gave him the news. Within the same hour, I called Terry. His response to the news was a genuine, "Aw, shucks."

We all remember the disgust and disappointment of that evening and how we each went to bed thinking we would just get through the funeral, then it would be every boy for himself. We thought maybe such independence would make us men.

To prevent the further escalation of tension between the families, we did not invite the Barnes family to the funeral. They found out about it on their own, though, and nicely sent multiple floral arrangements.

When we boys arrived at our mother's funeral, we saw the bouquets with the cards from the Barnes family members and panicked. Che and I quickly inspected each bouquet and took out all the cards from the Barnes family so that Grandma wouldn't know "the enemy" had infiltrated her baby's funeral.

When Grandma later examined every bouquet of flowers and wondered aloud why some had no cards, the four of us got a little chuckle out of how we had fooled her. In any case, Che and I congratulated ourselves on having averted a potential family feud flare-up. We later joked that had we not done that, Grandma would have lost her shit, and in the ensuing effort to restrain her, someone would have knocked over the closed casket and Mom's shriveled, disfigured corpse would have ended up on the floor of the church. That was about the only thing that could have made the funeral worse.

Even more than that dreadful funeral, I remember the rickety plywood box containing Mom's body at the crematorium, before they fed her into the furnace. The workers weren't used to people showing up at the warehouse where they burned the bodies, but it hadn't occurred to any of the brothers to let Mom go off into oblivion without us.

Just as they were about to feed Mom into the furnace, I asked for the box to be opened so I could take one last look at her. Looking a bit shocked by my request, a worker nevertheless approached the box with a crowbar, ready to pry the top off. He could, however, see the hesitation in my eyes.

"You sure?" he asked.

Then I thought, *No, I don't want to see her like this*. Then I thought, *Yes, I really should see her face one last time*, knowing the experience would be intense and real. I finally decided no. In that box, I would only have seen the decrepit, naked, bloated body of a woman with one breast, a plastic port coming from her chest, crumbled fingernails, a blistered face, and no hair. That body was no longer my mother. Mom had already become part of the cosmos.

Later, when I drove back to retrieve Mom's ashes, I placed the humble plastic urn in my truck's passenger seat and lovingly buckled the seatbelt over it for the ride home. I laughed a little to myself at this silly gesture, but as I drove, I kept looking over at the urn, checking on it, as if the idea of keeping Mom safe still had relevance.

Che, Noah, Freeman, and I, along with Mom's sister Debbie, took turns pouring Mom's ashes into a hole in a garden in front of the house, where we planted a purple locust tree. We set up a small boulder there, too, as a sort of tombstone, with Mom's name and dates and a sweet little saying engraved on it. But by this point, after the funeral and cremation, I had tired of ceremony. I think we all had. At least for me, these rituals did not ease the pain, so the planting of the ashes and tree wasn't much of an event. We just did it in a kind of exhausted way, but at least the four brothers did it together. This was the last thing we'd do together for a while. We had all been through too much and were ready for some space.

At this final ceremony, Aunt Debbie offered an unsolicited explanation for not having attended the funeral. She said the thought of flying coast-to-coast in a cramped airplane, knowing she was doing it for her beloved sister's funeral, was just too much to bear. Her explanation reminded me of Grandpa's sobs, and it struck me again that we were all simply taking care of ourselves at that point, coping with our own pain. None of us had anything left to give to anyone else. I was certainly there too.

Soon afterward, Che returned to his assignment flying Falcon jets for the Coast Guard in Puerto Rico. Noah returned to his work in San Francisco. Grandma and Grandpa returned to their home on the hill. Aunt Dianna returned to her home in Woodland, and Terry returned to tend his birdseed crop on his own farm nearby. The gathering at our farm, with everyone wanting to help or at least get underfoot, was over. Now, it was time for exodus.

I would soon return to college, but for the rest of that summer, I was the only adult around who could (supposedly) handle the farm's affairs until our new manager Chris took over in September. Taking on that thankless job for the time being made me realize anew, each day, exactly how little I knew about farming. To the extent that we had discussed selling the farm, we boys agreed we weren't ready, but that was all we could agree on.

Every day of that summer, I bumbled through a sincere attempt at being farm manager. Repeatedly, I pored over Mom's papers and notes, hoping to find the answers to innumerable questions. For instance, I had always taken for granted that crops made it to harvest, but now I had to figure out what crops to grow transplants for and which ones could be seeded directly into the ground. Furthermore, irrigation, fertilization, pest, personnel, office, and equipment issues all flowed directly to me. I directed the farm workers the best I could but stressed out over each decision and question. Afterward, I observed the results of my decisions to see if I had guessed right or wrong.

Besides the farm production issues, I got hammered by the outside world too. My produce was rejected for being in the wrong box. Buyers bullied me for better prices. The box supplier wanted to be paid *now*, even though he sold me the wrong boxes. Meanwhile, representatives from banks and insurance companies "casually stopped by" just to see if the place had fallen apart yet. One day, out of the blue, the Yolo County tax collector showed up unannounced, demanding an audit of our equipment list from which to increase our property taxes. The whole experience drained me so much that it felt like a challenge to my very existence.

As I muddled through, I remembered Mom openly contemplating whether or not she was doing the right thing by encouraging me to take on the farming business. No question about it: farming is hard. Maybe that's why she never fully explained the details of running this farm. Perhaps she thought knowing the truth would send me running for the hills. Indeed, it might have.

She had always encouraged us boys to pursue our own dreams. The farm was Mom's dream, but she didn't expect it to be ours. She would have loved it if one of us boys kept the farm going, but she had just never had the time to teach us. I should say to teach *me*, because Noah and Che definitely didn't want the job, and Freeman was too young. Farming is hard work, though, and honestly, if Mom had lived to a ripe old age, maybe we wouldn't have felt such an intense need to keep the farm alive. In that case, the farm would have run its course. But in July of 2000, the struggling farm was all of Mom we had left, and for Freeman and me, Capay Fruits & Vegetables was such a part of us that losing it would have felt like losing yet another parent.

The most important thing I had to do that summer was get the boxes for Farm Fresh To You, our community supported agriculture (CSA) program, packed and delivered. Money came in steadily from subscribers who believed in our farm and paid monthly to receive its local, organic produce. We could not disappoint those loyal customers. They were the most supportive group of people our farm had—more supportive, in fact, than the Barnes or Barsotti families.

So, while our relations indulged themselves in grief-filled isolation, my brothers and I scrambled to take care of the farm Mom had left us at the peak of harvest season. During this time, our mailbox was regularly filled with handwritten cards from our CSA members. Some offered condolences. Others shared specific memories of how Mom had touched their lives with her farm, its produce, and her recipes. Those expressions of sincere appreciation and gratitude gave me confidence and the resolve to keep the farm alive. They were nothing short of a North Star providing a clear path forward. Without them, the toil of Mom's life would likely have ended there, and her farm—along with the community supported agriculture movement it had helped found—would never have realized its full potential.

If I had flown back to Mexico and hid from the situation entirely, as part of me was inclined to do, our family legacy would have gone bust that summer. I don't think my brothers would have blamed me, though. I was only twenty years old, and no one else wanted the job. Running the farm had always been hard work, even for Mom, who knew how to do it. But I knew that even though Mom's death had made my world stop spinning, it had not done the same for the CCOF or the IRS or the many workers whose incomes relied upon the sixty acres we farmed at that time. Besides that, fields needed to be prepped, tomatoes needed to be harvested, taxes needed to be paid, paperwork needed to be completed, and our farmers' market stand needed to be manned. Noah volunteered to handle bookkeeping, Freeman took over running our farmers' market stand, and Che—out there in Puerto Rico—agreed to let us do whatever we wanted and basically stay out of farm affairs. That left me to act as interim farm manager. And away we went.

Me managing the farm myself, in the midst of profound grief, with no training but what I had learned from helping out Mom and Terry over the years, was a head aimed at a brick wall. Though nearly two decades old, Capay Fruits & Vegetables (we call it Capay Organic now) and our CSA Farm Fresh To You were like toddlers. You couldn't turn your back on either of them for a minute.

Case in point: I would find out later, the hard way, that Mom's death had already caused us to miss the last planting date for butternut, sugar pie, kabocha, and delicata—our winter squashes. If those seeds go in the ground after the Fourth of July, you can forget it. There aren't enough warm days of summer left to grow the crop to maturity. Who knew? I ended up planting them anyway. They looked great until October, when the weather cooled, and they only had tiny green fruit on their vines. The only thing we could do was disk acres of plants, with their shriveled little fruits, back into the earth. Money and time down the drain. Farming is all about growing and dying—but the trick is in the timing. Kind of like human life, I guess.

On the farm, our heirloom tomato crop, planted in the spring, had grown six feet tall by Mom's death in early July. Since ours are not the modern tomato varieties but old indeterminate varieties, they grow as vines and must be painstakingly trellised in order to give the tomatoes something to climb. So, once the plants are placed sixteen inches apart in five-foot-wide rows, and once they have established themselves in the earth, we pound six-foot-tall metal stakes into the ground every six feet of every single row and run string between the stakes, on either side of the tomato plants, training them up into acres of walls of tomatoes.

These are the numbers that tumble through a farmer's head every day: the distance to place plants apart, which determines the size of the fruit; the space between the rows, which is set by the wheel width of the equipment used in the region; the height of the stakes, which depends upon the expected length of the tomato vines; and the distance between the stakes, which is based upon the tensile strength of the string that must hold up the vines.

That summer, when I walked down the aisles between the walls of tomatoes, the scent of the field overwhelmed me. When I brushed lightly against a vine, a sticky green substance attached to my clothes and perfumed me. Inspecting tomatoes gave me a good workout, because I couldn't cut across the field and step over rows, like with eggplant, peppers, melons, and such. I had to walk all the way to the end of the row I was inspecting, then all the way down the next one. The only way out of the maze was to keep going forward.

The walls of tomatoes sometimes served as the perfect way to accidentally sneak up on unsuspecting wildlife. On one of these walks, I didn't even notice a mother turkey with her little poults nestled into the grass ahead of me. I must have been just a few feet away when she erupted into flight in an angry flurry of feathers.

I froze in place, chastened by her panic, while she landed in the tall, dry grass under a nearby oak tree. The little ones who had been hiding with her dashed around in circles, clearly unsure of the family emergency protocol. Some flew up over the tomato stakes and down into the next row. Others ran away from me down the length of the row. One stood completely still in hopes I would overlook him.

Adding to the madness of the moment, the mother turkey called loudly so her poults could find her. After a while, one by one, they scurried to her side. This chance encounter with me must have been highly stressful for the little family, indeed, but I admired the mother's quick thinking. She wouldn't always be able to protect her chicks, but for now, she was doing all she could. That was what Mom had done to the bitter end, and now this farm, and this family, had to find its own way without any guidance to speak of.

Chapter Two

·THE 1970s·

When Mom, on her deathbed, told me, "You haven't fallen in love, yet. That's fun!" I knew she was talking about her and Dad's initial courtship. Idealistic to the core, with a vision for a healthy new world, Kathy and Martin graduated from UC Riverside and entered graduate school at UC Davis during the wild and free 1970s. Inspired by their teachers and the back-to-the-land movement popular at that time, my mother and father wanted to build a better world right there, right then.

They began by asking local grocery stores to carry food grown without synthetic fertilizers, herbicides, or pesticides. The term "organic" didn't yet exist for this type of food. In fact, ever since the invention of farming with chemicals after World War II, very few people objected to these substances, which were considered an incredible sign of agricultural progress. After all, such chemicals made massive amounts of food available to feed the growing baby boomer population. But then, Rachel Carson published *Silent Spring*, all about how agricultural and other so-called "miracle" chemicals were destroying our environment. Throughout the 1970s, other seminal works of the environmental movement also brought to light the crisis being wrought by America's relatively new-fangled, chemical-heavy system of farming.

By the time my parents reached their idealistic twenties, a lot of people knew about how laborers on modern farms were exposed to chemicals that harmed their health. Some folks even knew about how America's emphasis on cheap, nonperishable food had tossed to the curb thousands of years of human crop selection in favor of tasteless "miracle" varieties. Such produce, bred to grow under the new chemicalized production system, was intended both for American use and to be shipped around the world.

When Mom and Dad asked grocery stores to carry all-natural produce, the stores just laughed at them. "Why would anyone pay extra for that stuff," they asked, "when what we have here is better and cheaper?" Still, my parents persisted in trying to improve our food system.

Next, along with some friends, they circumvented the grocery store system altogether and organized the Davis Farmers' Market, inviting local farmers to sell their wares directly to consumers. With the first market scheduled to take place, my folks became paranoid that nobody would show up, so they borrowed a quarter acre of land from the Beeman family. The Beemans liked the spirit of what my parents and their comrades were up to, so they agreed to let my parents—along with their friends Jeff and Annie Main and Henry Esbenshade—"farm" on that quarter acre of land. They agreed to name their little farm Good Humus and tilled every furrow themselves, laboring to create all-natural produce.

As luck would have it, Good Humus was able to grow a few bushels of the ugliest (but still delicious) produce anyone had ever seen, which they sold at the market. Soon, other local farmers also got excited about the idea. Many local farms—and, most importantly, local customers—showed up, so the Davis Farmers' Market was born. It soon spawned numerous additional farmers' markets throughout California. Over time, Dad established himself as part of the bedrock of the farmers' market community and regularly manned a stand that sold the tomatoes, peppers, melons, and squash he and Mom raised by hand with great love and care. The use of a little marijuana to inspire them didn't hurt either.

In 1974, Mom gave birth to the twins and brought them home to a double-wide at Barthel's Trailer Park in Davis. Shortly after the birth, Mom exclaimed in joy about her two perfect little boys, but Dad appeared less than thrilled at the prospect of being a parent. He walked out of the house, saying he needed "time to think." From that rough beginning, my father established a style of parenting light on nurturing.

Right away, it was obvious the twins weren't identical, or even alike. Mom named one boy Noah, for the great savior of humankind in the Bible. Dad named the other one Che, for Che Guevara, the great Marxist revolutionary and countercultural symbol of rebellion. This was well done, but they got the names backward. Che would turn out to be a kind, loving, intellectual leader of men and a commissioned officer in the United States military, whereas Noah, from the very beginning, was a rebel and hell-raiser who always challenged our parents.

As an example, when Che and Noah were about six or seven, they were playing near the barn one day. Rowdy Noah horsed around on a broken tractor while contemplative Che stared up at the sky, lost in thought. Che asked Mom a question about God, and she replied that God was in everything around us. In response, my sensitive, intellectual brother Che gazed in newfound wonder at the world, but incorrigible Noah, bouncing on the tractor, replied, "Then God's in this tractor seat, and I'm sitting on him!" That moment epitomized a difference between the two boys that would never change.

While my parents both finished their graduate degrees at UC Davis, they raised Noah and Che in the trailer park and continued to grow fruits and vegetables on that borrowed quarter of an acre, selling them at the Davis Farmers' Market.

For me, stories and memories are most often tied to the land, and I think of those few years farming that quarter of an acre as a precious time, even though I wasn't yet born.

It was there that my two older brothers locked themselves in the trunk of a car while everyone was transplanting crops. In another family story, Good Humus produced some spinach that was inadvertently contaminated with an unwanted herbicide, paraquat, from an agricultural aviator (they don't like being called "crop dusters" anymore). The herbicide tended to drift long distances from the intended application site, and in this case, it drifted over Good Humus and left yellow spots on the spinach that made it unsalable. The landowner, Howard Beeman, who had hired the agricultural aviator, told my dad the name of the airplane owner, prompting my dad to go to his office and confront him with three-year-old Che and Noah in tow, demanding fifty bucks for the spoiled product.

The man couldn't help but offer his opinion: "You're farming on Beeman's land, right where we used to dump buckets of DDT. You hippies should get out of Yolo County and do your farming up in the mountains, where it's safe." With that, he cut Dad a check, right there on the spot.

This was also the piece of land upon which my mother was first able to realize her knack for reviving interesting, long-forgotten crops such as sweet pea flowers and ambrosia melons. Dad later told us funny stories about how he and Henry Esbenshade used to go to "turn off the water" and take the opportunity to smoke weed in the truck before flipping the irrigation pump switch off. Most importantly, at Good Humus farm, these friends and colleagues discovered there was indeed economic value in farming chemical-free. Ironically, that value primarily came in the form of a gas tank on the farm that was kept full of the farmers' market proceeds, and everyone got to fill their vehicles from it.

This initial organic growers' movement not only attracted my parents' community of farmers, but also a widening circle of curious people interested in learning more about the cutting-edge idea of growing food without synthetic amendments. Our family stories always celebrated the shenanigans that arose from the unique combination of my parents' youth and idealism and nature's miraculous way of transforming soil, seeds, sun, and water into food.

My dad once confessed to me that this combination of factors led to his first encounter with the "free love" spirit of the time. A young woman came to the farm and immediately became enchanted with it. At that time, they were harvesting royal Blenheim apricots, and in the beginning, they ate more than they harvested. As they worked, the aphrodisiacs that are apparently found in apricots set in. By the end, the story goes . . . their appetites had shifted to each other!

The quintessential "idea guy," Dad was always coming up with schemes, some of which were really good ideas. Dad had his biggest, boldest idea when the twins were still just babies. He found twenty acres in the middle of nowheresville, Yolo County and suggested making the leap to actually living off the land instead of just hobby farming a borrowed quarter acre. Instead of being horrified by the isolation of the place, my mother jumped at the chance to raise their children out of the reach of civilization. She remembered her childhood in an Italian family, where a huge garden and annual grape harvest featured prominently. That's how my parents settled into Capay, California, in the mouth of the Capay Valley, making our farm the first organic farm in the Capay Valley. This twenty-acre patch of dirt would eventually become the place where I would be born and grow up. In fact, it would become the only place I have ever considered home. With the purchase, Mom and Dad left the Good Humus partnership for their newly founded farm: Capay Fruits & Vegetables. Meanwhile, Jeff and Annie Main continued to farm with the name Good Humus.

Second in importance to raising kids in their own little patch of paradise, Mom and Dad's goals included turning those twenty acres of yellow star thistle into an organic farm. By this point, Mom had an undergraduate degree in horticulture and a master's in statistics. Dad had earned his undergrad in psychology and master's in community development. So, they weren't complete dunces, but neither did they understand the business or lifestyle of being farmers. They knew no actual farmers at that time and had only grown a handful of different fruits and vegetables out there on Good Humus, on County Road 27, outside Davis. There, they had toiled extensively with the soil and grown enough viable food to sell, but it was nothing like what you'd call "living off the land."

First, though, Martin tried to get all their friends to buy nearby plots out in Capay Valley. Of course, his vision couldn't be limited to just our family, it had to include a whole community, potentially with cult status and the goal of taking over Capay Valley itself. Dad didn't just want to start a farm but a true organic food revolution. Like all his ideas, this one was big, Big, BIG! He sold the idea with his signature innate charisma and that twinkle in his eye that sometimes really mesmerized folks. He pitched the idea to anyone who would listen, even his father, who had a banker look at the plots. But the banker told Dad twenty thousand dollars for twenty acres was overpriced. This time, the only takers were Mom's parents, Frank and Lillah, who looked at the farming idea with skepticism but not despair. With Martin's permission, they bought the twenty acres across the street for a place to retire close to their daughter. That's how Grandma and Grandpa On-The-Hill ended up living across State Highway 16, which was then quite dreamily called "Star Route."

A charismatic visionary who challenged the status quo in everything he did, my father Martin could really rally people around a cause, but he also suffered from a certain lack of follow-through. Martin spent many years of his life working on our farm and selling its goods at farmers' markets, but he always seemed to view himself as above it all. Dad's dedication to providing for the family's financial stability was inconsistent, which made life stressful for Mom. So, while being a mother to little Noah and Che, Mom took on the role of primary bread winner too. During those early years, while Martin tinkered with his idealism, Mom worked as a researcher at UC Davis.

Throughout the 1970s, Dad did what he wanted, was a proponent of free love when it suited him, and enjoyed drugs while exercising very little responsibility. Mom's relationship with Dad was inspired by her desire to rebel from the strictness of her own father, a first-generation Italian used to working his ass off for everything he had. Mom's innate nature was not prone to doing drugs or lusting for random men, but she was young, too, and experimented with life along with Dad. Noah and Che remember a dude they used to call "Motorcycle Dan"—some guy who used to come around the house to see Mom. She tried to be a good sport about the free love thing for a while, but in her heart, she wasn't the same kind of revolutionary as Dad.

Decades later, I often heard both my parents refer to this phase of their lives. Mom, at the end of her life, looked back on it with regret. In fact, this era was a skeleton in her closet that followed her through life, and she advised us boys from her death bed "to always walk the straight and narrow." As for Dad, he once told me his generation gave my generation a lot of good things, "but free love wasn't one of them." He added: "Don't do it. It's bad news."

Dad loved us boys and supported whatever we wanted to do—the wilder, the better. Like a lot of counterculture leaders, Martin had an intoxicating way about him. He could paint pictures with words. He had, after all, used that skill to motivate Mom, a fellow idealist, to move to that twenty-acre yellow star thistle patch in the middle of nowhere, have more kids with him, and start an organic farm. Yet, he wasn't the type of man who could be counted on to build a farming business, share financial responsibility, or substantially help raise that family.

Throughout her twenties and thirties, Mom gradually realized that the bet she had made on her husband becoming more traditionally responsible with time was not going to pan out. With the passage of time, Dad remained the exact same kid she had married. He subjected her to an immense amount of stress in his pursuit for whatever it was he was after: his freedom, his "sticking it to the man," his being above the social norms that governed society. My mother was terrible at dealing with uncomfortable situations, and Dad was expert at creating them, so the conflicts between my parents just got worse over time and were never really resolved.

When it came time for Noah and Che to go to kindergarten, our parents—busy with the farm but also pretty inept at the whole parenting thing—figured they could just put their kids on the local school bus and trust the public school authorities of Esparto Unified School District to guide them from there. So, they waited with the boys at the end of the gravel driveway, then, when the school bus arrived, Mom and Dad boosted their confused little five-year-olds into the vehicle and waved goodbye. When the bus eventually stopped, Noah and Che got off with the rest of the kids but had no idea what to do from there.

They wandered around the school willy-nilly for an hour until someone found them and asked, "Who are you? Where are you supposed to be?"

The boys just shrugged.

This kind stranger figured out their classroom assignment, and, from there, everything went okay. The boys boarded the bus again that afternoon, returned to where Mom and Dad awaited them at the end of the driveway, and nobody was the wiser. Mom didn't find out about their little adventure for quite a while.

Those were our parents, though. They needed us to deal with a lot on our own from the very beginning, partly because that's just farm life, partly because Dad was not the coddling type, and partly because they were so busy with the farm they hardly had time to sleep, let alone parent. Over the years, they held high expectations of their children's abilities to work hard and look after themselves, just like Noah and Che on their first day of school. For the most part, we lived up to them.

Capay Valley was not a place that easily welcomed newcomers with different points of view. Its residents, for the most part, had inhabited this rural landscape for generations and were set in their ways. Despite being ninety minutes from San Francisco, Capay Valley was the epitome of rural America. Like any other place, this community had a variety of types of residents, but they all watched new folks with a wary eye. Credentials like college degrees and suburban upbringing were two strikes against entry to their club. In addition, the idea of farming without chemicals was something this rural community had never even contemplated. It's no stretch to say that, for many of the locals, this eccentric idea was the third strike against my parents. Though just forty-five minutes from UC Davis, which at the time was the center of all things revolutionary, my parents had found themselves in a foreign land. Ironically, UC Davis's agricultural program was still, at that time, a chemical-preaching institution.

Mom and Dad had the misfortune to move next door to a man named Johnny, who was infamous for not just cantankerous behavior but downright cruelty. Their relationship started friendly enough, though. In the beginning, my parents and Johnny and his wife Judy enjoyed friendly dinners together, but that ended when Johnny didn't like where my parents decided to put their driveway. To get my parents to move their driveway farther from his property, Johnny confronted my dad about the placement of the driveway in his own unique way: he stood just on his side of the property line and fired his shotgun several times into the air. Unfortunately, Johnny and my family were more than just next-door neighbors because Johnny owned land on three sides of our twenty acres. The only side he didn't own was where Highway 16 cut across, separating our land from Grandma and Grandpa On-The-Hill.

It became very clear that Johnny was none-too-pleased with having neighbors who were hippies, city folk, and university people. The fact that my parents completely fulfilled Johnny's doubts about them by having no idea how to run a farm only made things worse. An experienced conventional farmer, stuck in his ways, Johnny did everything in his power to drive my parents off the land and back to the city from whence they came.

Like most of the agriculture industry at the time, Johnny dismissed the organic foods movement as a bunch of bullshit. In fact, we later learned that behind my parents' backs, he used to dump his used motor oil onto our property, just to mock our concern for the environment. Several times, when one of our sprinklers wetted part of Johnny's gravel driveway, he walked into our field and smashed the sprinkler head with a baseball bat, leaving it to shoot water straight into the air and erode our crops wherever the random spray of water landed.

Johnny's most effective act of agricultural terrorism was to plant fast-growing eucalyptus trees along all three of the borders he shared with our land. These quickly grew very tall, blotting out our view of the valley as well as Johnny's view of us. The message was clear: *I don't want to see you. I'm going to pretend you don't exist.*

The USDA used to give out eucalyptus trees for use as windbreaks because they grow really fast, but they are a noxious, invasive species that ruin the view, block the sunlight, and prohibit anything from growing close to them. (Ironically, now the USDA assists landowners in getting rid of them.) With these trees, Johnny penned in our twenty acres in an effort to erase us.

My parents didn't understand cantankerous country people like Johnny, didn't own guns beyond a single-shot 0.22, and certainly didn't expect to have a hostile, feuding neighbor out there in what they had imagined would be a peaceful country setting. My mother was smart and strong but also somewhat easily intimidated, so Johnny—with his threats and dirty tricks—really got to her.

Johnny's favorite way to spread hate was through dogs. Even though he didn't hate dogs per se, he did hate people and knew he could make a lot of people miserable by tormenting a family's dog. Once, when our dog wandered onto Johnny's land, Johnny beat him viciously with a shovel. Our beloved black lab, Pup, limped home, cut and bleeding. That was when my parents realized Johnny wasn't just testing them. But, at that time, my folks had no proof against him, no rights if our dog had been trespassing, and no connections in Yolo County. So, having made their bed in this strange and threatening place, they slept in it as best they could.

In the country, there is a law (paired with a general neighborly understanding) that if a dog kills a rancher's livestock, the injured party can shoot the dog, no matter to whom it belongs. Technically, the dog needs to be caught in the act or on the property, but back then, the technical specifications of the law were unimportant details. It was the spirit of the law that mattered. So, Johnny used to go out of his way to let someone's dog loose from its kennel or leash. An hour later, he'd shove a wad of bloody wool in the dog's mouth and return it to its owners, pointing at the bloody wool as evidence that the dog had eaten one of his sheep. Then, he'd shoot the dog right there in the owner's yard.

Spreading hate was Johnny's game, and he never seemed to tire of it. Everyone in the community agreed the man was a first-class asshole, but he was not the only cranky old man out there in Capay Valley. My parents had simply bought property in the proximity of the most colorful of all of Capay Valley's feuding residents. No wonder the parcel had been so affordable.

Another Capay Valley resident, Gale, was paralyzed from the waist down due to polio he contracted while serving in the military. Thus, he had all his trucks and farm equipment altered so he could operate them with hands only. When my parents had only been in Capay for a few years, Gale went out to disk his field one day; meanwhile, he gave one of his grandkids a ride on the tractor. Disking is a way of tilling the soil with a heavy-bladed implement pulled behind a tractor. Somehow, the kid fell off the tractor and the implement ran him over, literally disking him into pieces, killing him. These kinds of tragedies happen on farms, sometimes. Next to Gale lived another colorful resident, Cliff, who was also handicapped, though less so. Cliff, who walked with the aid of a cane, was nicknamed "Borracho" throughout the valley ("drunk" in Spanish) because he was always drunk.

Now, I must preface the story about Gale and Cliff by explaining that, in the same way that some city folks are ridiculously obsessed with their lawns, some country folks spend way too much time and effort on their driveways. Gale was one of those guys. With his small, specially retrofitted front-end loader, he could easily manage the driveway's up-keep, and he enjoyed spending time and effort on keeping it tidy. To this end, each year, Gale would order a load of gravel and meticulously spread it around his house, up the drive, and along the easement past Cliff's house to the highway. Then, one day, Cliff—likely too drunk to notice or care what he was really doing—got inspired by Gale's activity.

Cliff hooked up his tractor with a grader in order to drag Gale's gravel onto his own driveway. Naturally, Gale blew his top over Cliff's bold gravel theft. This was just the type of thing Gale would stew on, endlessly. He called the sheriff, but upon arrival, the sheriff said there wasn't enough evidence for him to do anything. After all, one man's gravel looks just like another's.

Refusing to give up, Gale then tried to sue Cliff over the theft. When Cliff was served with papers, he became irate, picked up his cane, wobbled over to his truck, and drove the fifty yards down the driveway to Gale's house. At this point, Gale, all set to spar with his enemy, rolled to the doorstep in his wheelchair.

Remaining in his truck, Cliff shouted insults at Gale, who cursed back at him from his doorway. Then came the coup de grâce: at the height of the argument, Cliff stuck his cane out the window and pointed it at Gale. It wobbled here and there, as if shaky old Cliff were casting a spell on his neighbor. That's when Cliff called Gale a "baby killer," referring to the grandson he had accidentally disked into the Yolo County soil.

At that, Gale went crazy. He rolled his wheelchair across the front porch and grabbed the cane with which Cliff was taunting him. Cliff, deciding he had better get out of there, put his truck in reverse to back out of the driveway. Neither man let go of the cane, and Gale's wheelchair rolled with the truck across the newly graveled drive. The wheels of his chair got caught in the gravel that had been the source of all this fighting to begin with, and Gale flew out of his chair, into the gravel, and was dragged quite a few feet before he let go of the cane. That's Yolo County for you: even the physically disabled are mean sons of bitches.

Even though Yolo County did not turn out to be the utopia my parents had hoped, they still had their land, Mom's parents across the road, and their babies Noah and Che. During the seventies, my family fulfilled their dream of living off the land, growing enough food for themselves, and selling the rest of it direct-to-consumer at farmers' markets and to niche restaurants. My parents' original plan had never been to move to Capay and make a living growing fruits and vegetables. The idea was just to get the kids out of the city. Mom planned to hold down the finances with a real job, and Dad would tinker with upsetting the agricultural norm with the garden they shared. But one day, Mom realized that the cash Dad brought home from selling produce to fancy restaurants and at farmers' markets was more than her paycheck. This miraculous fact, coupled with an end to the funding for her job, motivated Mom to focus on the farm full time. When this change happened, the locals that often drove by the farm noticed a difference: the beds pulled through the fields were finally straight.

Noah and Che certainly were not city kids—the kind who go to lessons and afterschool activities every day and live in the thick of society. Instead, they learned to move irrigation pipe, dig potatoes, and amuse themselves by riding their bikes around the farm. Meanwhile, Mom and Dad struggled to learn the basics of farming and living in rural America. Overall, they were clueless about how all this country-living stuff really worked.

In 1980, Kathleen Barsotti gave birth to me, right there in the farmhouse. In true back-to-the-land hippie style, my placenta sat in a stainless steel bowl in the fridge for a week or two before they got around to burying it and planting a crabapple tree over it, right there in the front yard. Much later, whenever that bowl got put into use in the kitchen, Noah and Che (who remember repeatedly running into the placenta when searching the fridge for leftovers) used to tell me all about that disgusting memory. The fact that we continued to use that bowl daily became a sort of family joke. It eventually took on the role of designated barf bowl whenever someone was sick.

By the time I was toddling, my folks were not the only people in Yolo County likely to save a placenta in their fridge for ritual burying, but those few other hippie families in the area weren't really like our family. It's possible that Dad may have thrived working in partnership with the other organic farms that had come to the Capay Valley, but by this point, there was zero chance Mom would go along with their laid-back, hippie lifestyles. She was past that. She was a professional now. With Mom setting the tone for our farm and our lifestyle, we would never consider those new, hippie farmers "our people." By then, though, my parents were used to the fact that we did not fit into Yolo County and were long past caring.

Chapter Three

·AUGUST 2000·

Only days after Mom died, our farm workers expected paychecks. As much as these folks sympathized with our family, I knew they couldn't afford to stick around unless their money arrived on time. This being the height of harvest season, other local farms would eagerly snap up our workers and leave us with tomatoes rotting in the field, so I sat down at Mom's desk and tried to make sense of things.

Our office staff of two understood some managerial items but knew zip about others. Mom had always done the important stuff herself, so when I tried to do payroll, the office staff only gave me blank stares. Most of my questions were met with the honest answer, "I don't know, Thad. Kathy always did that." Along with each payroll batch, I had to pay what I owed to Uncle Sam, so each time I sent the government a check, I also filled out a neat little form for the IRS, where I had to check a bubble that corresponded to the type of payroll tax: either 941 or 943. I dutifully went through it all, step-by-step, blacking in the 941 bubble each time, paying the taxes, and filling out the IRS form.

I followed all the IRS instructions to a T, or so I thought. Each time, the government deposited my checks, and each time, I thought about how ridiculous it was for me to spend my time paying these taxes on a farm my family was on the verge of losing. I only wanted to focus on keeping Capay Fruits & Vegetables, the last connection I had with my mother, from crumbling to nothing. It annoyed me that number-two pencils and Excel spreadsheets were turning out to be more important tools for this than shovels or welders. Despite my diligent bubble filling and form writing, I soon received a certified letter from the IRS. Then, another and another arrived. There seemed to be no end to them.

The first "friendly" reminder prompted me to check if the IRS was depositing my checks. It was. The second, in a menacing tone, directed me to pay what I owed to the IRS. The third was a registered letter that informed me that since Kathleen Barsotti was not paying taxes, the agency was preparing to repossess the farm and everything Kathleen Barsotti owned.

That one jolted me to move this to the top of the priority list. I didn't know much about compliance at the time, but I knew not paying the IRS was a sure way to start with an inheritance and end up with nothing. I remembered how the father of one of my childhood friends told me that, in defiance of the Vietnam War, he had calculated how much of his taxes were going to the war and refused to pay that share of his taxes. The IRS did not think it was funny. They put him in jail. Admittedly, there was a lot I didn't know, but from that story, I knew not to mess with the IRS, so I called the phone number provided.

"I have a problem I need some help with," I said. "I'm paying the taxes and filling in the forms. You're depositing the checks, but you've sent me this letter saying I'm not paying the taxes. What do I need to do to fix this?"

"Are you Kathleen Barsotti?" asked a cold voice on the other end of the line.

"Funny story," I replied. "She recently died. I'm her son who just took over her responsibilities."

"We can only talk to the person named on the account," said the robotic man, who may as well have hung up on me but instead let me waste my time pleading my case before saying no.

Here, the IRS had been receiving checks from Kathleen Barsotti for the past few months, gleefully cashing them, and never caring at all that she was dead. Now it mattered? It didn't help that Noah and Che were the official executors of Mom's trust, so I couldn't legally claim to be a representative of the trust. Still, I was the one writing payroll checks and filling in IRS forms. Whatever there was to know, I was the only one who knew it.

A sophomore engineering student, I didn't know much about business, but I did know that the farm had never been made into a business entity. It had always been simply a sole proprietorship, and now it was even less than that. It was in the gray area where a sole proprietor had turned it into a revocable trust. Mom's social security number was the owner of the twenty acres and the cashless checking account until some unknown point in the future when the trust would stop. As far as the IRS was concerned, Capay Fruits & Vegetables was a woman, who happened to be dead, growing vegetables and owing taxes. End of story.

On top of that, the man from CCOF, our organic certifier, hounded me nearly every day about a set of paperwork items he needed. He was so intense about it that you would think I had turned the farm into a testing site for Monsanto's GMOs.

In the midst of this, I would go to bed every night and have a recurring dream about being in a white room with picture frames on the walls. Mom inhabited the pictures inside the frames but jumped from one frame to another, randomly, while I asked her what to do about all the troubles on the farm. In each dream, I described in detail whatever problem I happened to be grappling with at the time. From inside one of the frames, Mom would always begin talking, and the suspense would build, like the way it does when a contestant on *Jeopardy!* is about to answer a question. Then, just as Mom was about to provide the definitive answer I so desperately wanted, the dream would abruptly end, and I would wake up incredibly frustrated.

Lying in bed awake, I used to ponder why Mom wasn't giving me the answers from wherever she was in the cosmos. Surely, I thought, she could have figured out how to help me by now! Slowly, with each unanswered question in this dream, my faith in the afterlife dissipated.

I really wanted to believe Mom was out there, watching over me, in some medium I could comprehend, but I knew that if she were, she would give me the damn answers. Nothing would stop her. Now I realize the dreams were simply memories of my mother surfacing from my subconscious, minus the knowledge I sought. It was torture to realize that, in me, Mom was still alive to some degree but not alive enough to give me those important answers. Slowly but surely, night after night, my new reality settled in: I was alone with all the farm's problems.

At one point that month, I heard a rumor from the crew about a turkey at the edge of a certain field who still had a clutch of eggs in a nest. There's something magical about seeing a nest full of warm eggs almost ready to hatch, so I followed the directions I had been given. Standing at the base of the oak tree where I was told the nest lay, I couldn't find anything, so I did what Che had once taught me.

Working Search and Rescue for the Coast Guard, he found lost things and people all the time, and he did it by simply dividing the area into a grid and searching each square, one at a time. For instance, once, Noah lost his engagement ring in the irrigation canal, and we all figured it was gone forever. Not Che. He parked a van along the canal where Noah lost the ring, tied himself to the van with a rope to avoid fighting the current, and entered the canal. Wearing a diving mask, he imagined a grid across the area in question and searched each square, looking up the first column of squares, then down it again, then over to the next column, and again searching up and down. BINGO, he saw the shiny thing sitting on the edge of a crack in the canal's concrete side.

Thinking of that, and eager to find the mother turkey that I knew to be somewhere nearby, I built my own imaginary grid around the area. Standing perfectly still, I visually searched each square thoroughly. Still . . . nothing.

Finally, when I had given up on finding her, I noticed a shiny thing in the grass, like a BB. I stooped to take a closer look and realized it was the hen turkey's eye. She had been right in front of me all along, but her brown feathers camouflaged perfectly with the twigs and leaves. She knew I was there. She might have even known I was looking for her, but she wouldn't let fear make her abandon her babies. That hen was not getting off her nest for anything. Thinking of Mom, and how distraught she had been about leaving my brothers and me, I wondered (despite my creeping doubt in the afterlife) if, like that hen, my mother was there, too, somehow hidden in the twigs and leaves of the farm.

During those summer months, I talked to Ricardo, our foreman, in my brand-new Spanish, communicating certain things I knew needed to be done. He would also communicate things he knew to me, but I wasn't up to the level of a native Spanish speaker. These laborious conversations often involved very specific, technical vocabulary I hadn't learned at my language school or travels through Mexico. The only thing I knew for sure was that Thaddeus is Tadeo in Spanish, and I was known to every Spanish-speaking person on the farm as Tadeo. During some of these early conversations, I often wasn't sure if we had just agreed on what I meant to say or the exact opposite, but at least I got my own name right.

Slowly, though, my confidence built, until one day, I heard one of the workers, in Spanish, tell another farmer who had come to deliver some produce: "Hey Jeff, you've been trying to speak Spanish your whole life, but Tadeo goes to Mexico for three months, and now he speaks better than you!"

Victory!

In hindsight, my grasp of Spanish was the very key to keeping the farm alive that summer. Even though my Spanish wasn't very good, I could achieve basic communication with the workers, and that made all the difference. This was the one "superpower" I had. Each week, I learned more about what the outside world needed from our farm, such as heirloom tomatoes and forecasts of the harvests we would be able to provide for each variety. Instead of trying to do this myself, I could translate these requests to the crew. Then, like magic, a slip of paper would appear in my hand with accurate estimates, thus enabling me to liaise with the outside world and keep doing the farm's business. This exchange went the other way too. I functioned as the crew's connection to the outside world, making supplies and services show up so they could do their jobs. Without this flow of information, the farm would have shriveled up like a plant with a girdled stem choking it to death.

Mom's death had certainly done nothing to slow down tomato growth, so despite everyone's grief, we harvested heirloom tomatoes like gangbusters throughout August. On top of that, lemon cucumbers, sweet peppers, Japanese eggplant, sweet one-hundreds, sungold cherry tomatoes, ambrosia and galia melons, opal and Italian basil, mission figs, sweet peaches, and okra rounded out our farm's offerings to Farm Fresh To You customers. In the orchards beyond the fields, our satsuma mandarins were also sizing quickly, reminding us that summer would soon end, and fall was near.

Ricardo seemed to have a handle on the ongoing harvests, but this month we also had to attend to seeding fields for the next harvest and transplanting seedlings from our greenhouses. It is never simple on a farm. You must manage the future even as you catch up with the demands of the present. Like me, Ricardo had taken orders from Mom. He didn't know—had never needed to know—the planting schedule by heart.

I knew the seeding had to be done on a very specific schedule, but for the life of me, what was it? As far as I could tell from the research I did in Mom's office, she kept that information in her head. I did manage to find neat, handwritten lists of the seed orders, but that was just a tease and made it even more frustrating that I couldn't find what I really needed. The only other person who would know Mom's planting schedule was Terry, but Terry and I weren't talking much. Sadly, with Mom's death, a chunk of my relationship with Terry died too. It all had to do with Terry's weirdness around money.

For instance, soon after Mom's funeral, while I was in the midst of dealing with the IRS and the CCOF, I received a sizable surprise bill from the funeral home. I immediately called Terry, who had told everyone in the family he would cover the expense himself and made a big deal about it. At the time, I had found this offer rather strange, knowing how tightfisted Terry normally was. Turns out, I was right to be concerned. Not wanting to double-pay the bill, I called and asked Terry if he had already paid the funeral bill, like he said he wanted to. Terry told me he had changed his mind because he didn't think he had been treated properly in Mom's last days or at the funeral. At the time of that fateful call, the farm was still borrowing some of Terry's farm equipment, as Mom had done for years. So, while we were on the phone, Terry also reminded me of this fact, slyly suggesting that I owed him for the equipment. I was stunned, but all I could do was roll my eyes. The idea that I was still a kid and the adults in my life would help me in any way was gone. Everyone was looking out for themselves now.

The more I thought about it, though, I realized Mom had removed Terry as the executor of her trust for a reason. He could be controlling in exactly this way, using money, or the lack of it, instead of words, to communicate whether he was happy or upset. His behavior was strange, but thankfully I recognized it for what it was: manipulation. This was something I knew I needed to cut from my life.

At another point in time, when Terry and my brother Noah met with our accountant to deal with some miscellaneous items, Terry told the accountant in front of Noah, "Well, we can always figure that out during the deposition."

When Noah mentioned this to me later, I didn't know what to think, as I didn't even know what a deposition was. Noah explained it's part of the process of a lawsuit. I chalked the statement up to yet another money-strange-Terry comment. Making manipulative comments about suing us boys, despite having nothing to sue us over, was exactly his style. So, just a month and a half after Mom died, Terry was the last person I wanted to call to ask about Mom's planting schedule.

I can now confidently state that the appropriate plantings for late summer would have been only vegetables that harvest in the fall: bok choy, beets, radishes, spinach, kales, chards, lettuces, fennel, cilantro, parsley, cabbage, broccoli, cauliflower, and carrots, but I didn't know that then. I looked around, noticed the Capay heat, and figured it was so hot we could still grow *anything*, including tomatoes, melons, peppers, and winter squash. I didn't realize that, including all of August, there were only forty-five days left of hot summer days and warm summer nights before the fall weather would roll in, delivering nighttime lows in the forties and only a few hundred-degree highs. Summer crops like tomatoes, melons, peppers, and winter squash need 60 to 120 days of summer weather, depending on the crop. These are all things I learned the hard way.

Most of the summer crops we planted that year were destined to yield nothing. They would grow beautifully in August, then slow in September and October. By November, it would be obvious that all we had done was pay money to grow fruitless plants that would die in the cooler weather. We timed a few crops correctly, but even with these, we had another problem to contend with: seeder settings.

To plant with a seeding machine, one must carefully select the right-sized plate that matches the seed size so that each hole only grabs one seed. The farmer must adjust certain gears to determine the exact linear distance between each individual seed drop. That's assuming you sized the seeder plates correctly, so that you drop one seed, not zero, two, three, or four seeds. All these sizes and spaces need to be determined for each seed of each different vegetable variety. All of this also requires specialized seeding equipment, of which we had very little.

Put seeds too far apart, and the field is wasted on half a crop while the fruit grows too big and leaves room for weeds to flourish. Too close together, and the seedlings crowd each other out, resulting in fruit that's too small. Using a gear that's too big puts too much seed out with each drop, forcing too many plants to compete for the same real estate. These little decisions are crucial to making the farm pay for itself, which, at that point, was still a pipe dream.

I scoured the notebooks in Mom's office and was lucky enough to find one where she kept track of her experimentation seeding the different vegetables. It seemed carrots were always problematic, and she still hadn't mastered them. I drew pictures of vegetables and their corresponding gears for Ricardo, so there would be no misunderstandings. He could simply compare the gear I drew to the actual gear to which he would attach that particular drive chain.

While I was confident in my ability to read, write, and speak enough Spanish to communicate these things, Ricardo—who hailed from a farm in a tiny pueblo called Jesús María in the Mexican state of Jalisco—was illiterate in Spanish as well as English, having had no formal education. The pictures worked, though, as a method of communication, and he was a smart man, able to figure things out. With this, we designed a system to communicate our plan, but it still didn't work. The seeding equipment was old, and even if we got the spacing right, the beds were too cloddy to foster good germination. In the few cases where the beds were smooth and the seed spacing right, we more often than not lost the crop to thick weed pressure. The only solution to this was for me to exercise my budding managerial skill and hire a crew to hand weed the crop, which ended up costing so much money that we had no chance of making any profit. It would take Ricardo and me years to get this all figured out, so it's safe to say that first fall was, quite simply, a genuine mess.

The other fall crops—like kales, chards, lettuces, and cauliflower—go into the ground not as seeds but as seedlings started in greenhouses, so we needed to transplant those seedlings as well. This was not as hard to determine, since a stroll through the greenhouses showed me which plants were already getting leggy and needed to go into the ground. Getting the right seeds into their flats in the greenhouse was one thing that Mom had been able to do for me before she passed. Machines exist for planting transplants but buying one of those seemed financially unfathomable for us. So, like always, we got a field crew to perform the task by hand and eventually got it done. The beauty of transplanting is that the plants are already relatively big, so that gives us a chance to outgrow the weeds in the field and actually cultivate a crop.

Around this time, I thought I must have gotten a weird allergic rash, because the skin on my hands was peeling, like skin does after a bad sunburn. But the peeling got worse and worse until the skin on every inch of my palms and fingers sloughed off in layers like the bark of a sycamore tree. I went to a dermatologist who gave me some moisturizing cream that did nothing except make a paste out of the dead skin.

Later, when I returned to the clinic, convinced I had contracted something terrible, I got a new doctor who was significantly more competent than the last. She examined my hands, looked me in the eyes, and asked, "Can you think of anything going on in your life right now that might be causing you stress?"

I couldn't help but chuckle. "Yeah, I can think of a few things," I replied.

"Some people react to stress this way. You should try to relax," she said.

I looked at her funny, wondering how in the world I was going to relax at the peak of harvest season. I just responded, "Okay, I'll work on that."

To this day, I use my hands as a forward indicator of how much stress is in my life. When the tips of my fingers start to peel, I know I need to make some changes.

That August, Ricardo and the others brought in the tomato harvest. It was a flush, meaning a hell of a lot of one thing that we had to harvest immediately and sell quickly. August in Yolo County's Capay Valley can run above one hundred degrees, and those hot tomatoes needed to be shoved in the cooler right away after harvest to take them from close to a hundred degrees to closer to fifty or sixty. This was necessary to remove the field heat so that their ripening would slow enough to make it to the customers before they were too ripe. Unfortunately, we only had one cooler for all of it, so that meant: harvest it, cool it, and sell it lickety-split to make room for the tomatoes coming in the next day. And sell them we did.

By the summer of 2000, Mom had developed her heirloom tomato crop into practically an art form. Our heirlooms were now planted for a wholesale market. So, each night, a twelve-pallet bobtail truck, operated by a third party, would pull up the driveway, and we would pack twelve pallets of tomatoes, cooled from their field temperature, into the truck destined for our wholesale marketer, Peter, at Earl's Organic who had them all sold to an up-and-coming retailer, Whole Foods Market. This system was a big, recent change for our farm. Never had we produced such a profitable cash crop that we could sell wholesale. Meanwhile, I worried that the Farm Fresh To You customers were getting sick of having so many tomatoes in their home-delivered boxes.

A couple of weeks before Mom died, she showed me a handwritten list on a half sheet of paper. This was how she communicated what went into the next week's box. First, she listed stuff from our farm; second, she listed stuff from other farms that complemented our selection. At the end of the process, there was a certain amount of money that should be spent per box, and the mix of products needed to be good.

Since I didn't ask her anything about it, she protested, "You should pay more attention to this!"

I remember responding, "Mom, picking what goes into the Farm Fresh To You box isn't that hard. You look at what our farm has, then you add stuff from other local farms to make a good mix, and don't spend too much money."

She laughed and agreed. I like to think the foolish confidence I showed that day made her feel better about the inevitability of me managing the farm for a few months after she died. While there was a lot of information about running the farm that Mom never got to share with me, I had picked up quite a lot through a childhood spent harvesting and hustling each season's product at the farmers' market. So, I knew the farm's seasonal products and what sold well.

Now, I was the mom of the farm and had the job, every week, of deciding how many melons, eggplants, peppers, and heirloom tomatoes to put into the boxes and what to buy from other farms. I admit, it was harder than I had anticipated. At that time, I thought variety was the main appeal of getting home-delivered, local produce, so in my zeal to please customers, I excluded tomatoes sometimes and loaded the boxes with more of the other vegetables and fruits.

Finally, I received an angry letter from one of our CSA customers, asking, "Why, at the height of summer, am I not receiving tomatoes in every box? It's tomato season! I expect tomatoes!"

The reprimand upset me, but after some soul searching, I realized the customer was right. Our members didn't want variety, like you can get at a grocery store. They wanted to eat with the seasons. If we grew a flush of tomatoes, our Farm Fresh To You customers were happy to take the excess off our hands. I had been overthinking the whole thing! In this way, and so many others, our CSA members helped me learn on the job.

The next week, I generously loaded the boxes with tomatoes, among other produce, and once again, all our loyal customers were happy. Meanwhile, at the farmers' market, Freeman made short work of selling the melons we also harvested in August. One way or another, food came in off the field and got to its intended buyers before it was too late, but every day I worried we wouldn't pull this off. Every night, that worry kept me awake unless I personally saw to it that the whole-sale truck was loaded, then watched it physically leave the farm.

With the next payroll I sent out, I called the IRS back to continue trying to solve the tax problem. By now, I had received yet another certified letter. This time a new but equally cold voice on the other end of the line repeated that if I was not Kathleen Barsotti, I was not privy to her confidential financial information. *Click!*

I found it incredible that these people hung up so glibly on the grieving son of their deceased taxpayer. The IRS was certainly living up to its heartless reputation. Every time I called, I talked to someone new. So far, they all managed to be completely unwilling to help at all; some while talking in a weirdly friendly tone.

One hot August night, those twelve-hour days of confusion, seat-of-the-pants decision-making, numerous failures, and IRS problems to top it all off got to be too much for me. With the last truck out, I had a moment for myself. In the moonlight, at the little tree that marked my mother's grave, I broke down sobbing into my peeling, disintegrating hands. I begged Mom for guidance and bellowed through my sobs, "I don't want to do this!" It was all too much.

The next morning, desperate, I called the IRS again and got yet another operator. I explained the situation and my confusion about it yet again, insisting that I had been paying the requisite taxes all along. This lady, for some reason, chose to overlook the technicality of me not being Mom and tapped away on her computer. After a few minutes of her checking into the depths of the IRS system, she said, "Oh! It looks like you have excess payments in the 941 account and deficient payments in the 943 account. We can just switch the funds over."

Finally, a government employee with some common sense and empathy!

Apparently, I should have been filling in the bubble for 943 (required annual reporting for agriculture) instead of the 941 (required quarterly reporting for most business). For that error, I came a hair's breadth from having the farm seized by the IRS.

That August of 2000, having solved the great and trenchant mystery of the 941 versus 943 IRS bubble, I finally relaxed, one sweat-drenched August evening, on the deliciously cool terracotta tile of the living room floor. As Freeman and I lay there, sweltering and staring at the ceiling, we listened to the honking of Canada geese passing overhead in their annual migration. It was a sign that, thank God, fall weather loomed.

Once, as a kid, I stood in a field while a formation of geese flew so close overhead that I could hear the air rushing over their thousands of feathers. I waved my arms at them, made the leader flinch, and the whole flock flinched with him. Back then, I could never just marvel at nature but had to see how close I could get to it before it reacted and acknowledged me. Lying on the cool tile, just listening, I felt glad to have outgrown that.

That evening, I finally explained to Freeman what I had been worried about the past few weeks, showed him my corroding zombie hands, and told him this was a syndrome from stress. Freeman was shocked. Ever since Mom's death—well, since long before that, actually—we had both been wrapped up in our own little worlds, hardly thinking about the other.

In a matter of weeks, school would start for each of us, and we would be back to obsessing on our individual mountains of work, but at least for this one evening, we could relax and try to be brothers again. It was weird, though, without Mom in the next room.

The next morning, I dressed in my farm uniform: boots, jeans, long sleeve button-up shirt, and ball cap. All the farm workers had developed their own uniforms that specifically fit their jobs. The office folks had the luxury of being able to wear open-toed shoes and shorts as they escaped the heat in the air-conditioned office, but the field crew wore the most clothing in summer. They understood from experience that protection from the sun is the best way to keep up your energy when spending a full day in the ruthless Capay heat. Their heavy work uniforms of boots, jeans, and hooded sweatshirts with the hood on, coupled with jugs of drinking water, prevented sunburn, dehydration, and scratches.

By this point in August, the leaves of the oaks all around the farm had long ago turned from springtime's mint green to a mature olive color. Noticing this change in the early dawn light reassured me that the summer's oppressive heat would soon break, rain would come, and with it the end of the year's most intense harvest season. In the distance, a tractor planted the last of the summer squash nearby the winter squash field. I still didn't realize the winter squash had already gone into the ground too late, so I saw potential in the emerging green shoots of what appeared to be a healthy crop.

Being a farmer isn't like any other profession. It's not as nomadic of a skill as many might think. I couldn't move to another place in the world and apply everything I learned the hard way in Capay for a successful first season. Depending upon the latitude, altitude, and season length—which is often a function of proximity to ocean, desert, or mountain—planting dates like that for winter squash could change radically. My knowledge of this land, hard won as it has been, is specific to this little part of the world, located in California's Yolo County, near the town of Capay, population 200, elevation 250. Having learned the hard way in Capay, I'm sure I would learn more quickly in another place, but it would still take years to farm well in a new area.

With Mom's twenty acres of tomatoes almost all harvested, I felt like everyone on the farm drew a collective breath. A sense of relief washed over me when I saw the cooler empty for a day, instead of having it constantly piled high. Over time, this farm had managed to turn heirloom tomatoes into cash left over in the bank account, but the stress of having to sell so many at once made me happy to say goodbye to the year's biggest profits and the worry that came with it.

Mom had been right: twenty acres of heirlooms was a hell of a lot to plant. If Mom's and my plan to manage the harvest together had worked out, it would have been achievable without losing too much sleep, but with just me, it was a miracle I wasn't sitting on a pile of rotten tomatoes at that point.

Walking beside Cache Creek one morning, I noticed that one newly seeded field looked so pristine the dirt seemed clean, like I could eat off it. I recognized Ricardo's workmanship. Indeed, I spied him in the distance on the green John Deere pulling an orange seeding implement. What he had done here was to first apply a few tons of compost (organic fertilizer), then mulch the field with a machine resembling a giant rototiller, which broke up large dirt clods and mixed in the fertilizer. That made everything nice and smooth and even. Afterward, he dragged the seeder along each planting bed, depositing the seeds at the exact distance and depth for which the machine had been set. This was the one setup that we had found to work. It planted the big winter squash seeds and did a decent job.

Easing down a furrow between seed beds, I squatted, pulled out a pocketknife, and prodded the earth just enough to uncover a squash seed three-quarters of an inch down. This is where farmers become like tailors, measuring things down to an eighth of an inch. It would be nice if we could just throw some seeds into the soil and skip off into the sunset. Instead, we shake our heads in disappointment if a seed is buried a fraction of an inch too deeply or shallowly.

In this case, I felt the squash seed may have been a touch too deep but was still within the safe range—the danger being that the delicate little sprout could run out of energy before breaking the surface of the soil and gaining the ability to photosynthesize. If it didn't get sun soon enough, its little life would fizzle out before a single leaf could form. Then again, burying a seed too shallowly ran the risk that the sprout could dry out before its root established a water source.

The next thing I should have checked was the spacing between seeds, but back in 2000 I had no idea how to judge this or how very crucial each inch of separation was. I knew so dreadfully little then. Over time, I would come to realize that each patch of soil held a finite amount of energy. In a good field, a farmer can evenly distribute this energy to each plant or piece of fruit in the field. Seed spacing is the very thing that determines how big each plant or piece of fruit gets: the higher the number, the smaller the fruit. A lower density makes larger fruit.

Regarding the elements of sunlight, soil temperature, and drainage, farmers have no control at all. We have some control over elements like water and nutrients, but seed spacing and plant dates are the main things we can control. If we master this art, we grow a crop that is salable in the marketplace. If not, we're at nature's mercy. In school, they teach all kinds of methods to figure out the best mix. In real life, we use a series of educated guesses.

In time, I would learn that on a sixty-inch-wide bed, one line of seeds spaced fifteen inches apart, seeded directly into the ground after the middle of April but before the middle of June, gave the winter squash fruit the right amount of resources to grow to the correct size in enough time in the Capay summer heat to take the squashes to maturity. I wish farming were so simple that "big" always fit the bill, but in truth (I learned the hard way) farm-to-table restaurants, wholesalers, retail stores, and even individual families tend to prefer smaller, two-pound winter squashes. That's a perfect size for a family meal, thus the most salable size. Luckily for us, we had our faithful Farm Fresh To You members, who accepted whatever size squash we produced. They were more interested in knowing the source of their food than in having the food be of a standardized size and shape. I think starting the CSA and thereby finding the right kind of customers to appreciate a farm like ours—that was probably Mom's greatest accomplishment.

Sadly, my first crop of butternut squash would end up being too messed up even for my devoted Farm Fresh To You customers. Planted too late, the fruits would be stillborn. Squash needs the heat to grow, but fall days cooled off and doomed the crop. The following season, when the farm would finally produce a field of viable butternut squashes, I would think them beautiful as newborn babes. Now, I have coined a little saying reminding me when the end of the planting window for winter squash approaches: squash should be "knee high by the Fourth of July," otherwise, you've missed the window. Every year when I know the Fourth of July is approaching and see I the first fireworks stands go up, it reminds me that I had better have my winter squash well on its way.

Those first years of farming without Mom, Noah nagged me endlessly that it was impossible to sell my "nasty, big-ass butternuts" to wholesalers. Literally, he could not give them away. It would take several seasons of going back to the drawing board—finally planting the seeds both on time and much closer together—to grow squashes that met the unyielding standards of produce retailers.

That August, when things were really busy, we didn't have enough trucking to get our product to the city, so I found myself driving our four-hour delivery runs of produce, usually after a full day's work. Once, on one of those runs, at a truck stop, I saw an old man sitting in a car. He looked so very old that I thought, *that man will probably die soon.* I envied him. How wonderful it would be, I thought, to relax into certain oblivion, knowing there was nothing else to do, nobody who counted on you, no deadlines to make. I caught myself and realized what a weird thought this was, but that was the state I was in that August.

Starting the following month, these deliveries would become our farm manager Chris's problem. I would return to studying agricultural engineering, and, from there, probably become a civil engineer. After that, who knew? Few with that major ever actually go into farming. I didn't know what the future held. I just wanted to check off this box called "college" and move on and become an adult. More than anything, I wanted to find my own way and not be dragged back down into spending my life on this farm with its endless chores and meager pay.

On the tail of August, at the end of a long, hard day of doing deliveries, I stretched my legs with a walk along the canal and eventually took shelter in the shade of an oak tree bordering a field. Sweat soaked, I marveled at how much shelter the tree gave me. Of course, I had noticed this phenomenon before, but it never really ceased to amaze me. In the shadow of the oak's thick blanket of leaves, my eyes could relax from the summer glare and my skin no longer felt assaulted by the sun's rays. One step outside that shadow, though, and August's heat wave hit me full force.

Intellectually, I knew September would bring the refreshing cool of fall, but in the heat of summer it was hard to imagine how quickly things would change on our little piece of the planet, as the earth continued its revolution around the sun.

Chapter Four

·EARLY 1980s·

On a cold, rainy night in February, when I was about five or six, Mom once picked up the phone and took an order for baby turnips. Chez Panisse, a farm-to-table restaurant in Berkeley, needed these the next day for their seasonal menu. Mom sent Noah, Che, and me out to the field to dig up turnips at dusk like a bunch of druids doing some weird ceremony. I remember how cold my little fingers were as I dug in the rain, in the earth, for the round, radish-sized roots. Our directive was to dig up one thousand turnips, each about the size of a quarter. This daunting task was made more difficult by the sticky-clay Tehama silt loam soil of the land my parents had chosen to homestead.

When you're a kid playing in the creek in the summer sunshine, it feels like it's always sunny. But when you're digging in the cold, wet mud, you feel like it's always rainy and miserable. I remember, as a kid, having no sense of the future or the past like I do now. Every moment felt like all there was. If I felt terrible, life was drudgery, and I couldn't remember life ever being different. If I felt great, life was a picnic, and that was all I could imagine.

That night, life was a shivering cold hell you couldn't escape until you counted out *one thousand* turnips. Yet, in our work, my brothers and I shared a certain camaraderie. This order for turnips meant hours on the "earn card," our handmade record-keeping system. In theory, those hours would eventually turn into money.

As each boy pulled up handfuls of turnips, he would toss out the babies and count the quarter-sized ones into a disheveled, old produce box that was on its second or third use.

"One hundred and seven! One hundred and eight!"

"Ten more! One hundred and eighteen!"

We dug and dug, occasionally observing where the turnips had been planted too close together and were therefore too small to use. We rejoiced when we found a patch where they had been planted just right, and we could gather ten or twenty good ones at once.

Eventually, someone shouted, "That's eight hundred even!"

"Eight hundred and three!"

"Eight twenty-three!"

The pain in our fingers that evening built up, but as the count climbed toward one thousand, the feeling that this would go on for the rest of our lives dissipated. In the distance, we could see the light on in the kitchen window. There, Mom and Dad took care of baby Freeman and cooked something whole grain and healthy for dinner. The smell of the smoke emerging from our chimney reminded us that every square inch of this farm was not miserable. The comforts of home would be ours just as soon as we hit that thousand-turnip mark.

Eventually, we trudged home, covered in mud, rocks in our shoes, pulling a cart stacked with mismatched, reused produce boxes containing the results of our hard labor.

In the light of the front porch, Dad turned on the hose and sprayed off the dirty cart, and we brought handfuls of turnips into the house. But that was not the end. After all that time in the mud, there was still more work to be done.

"Be careful of the leaves!" Mom warned.

The leaves had to stay attached. You don't eat the leaves, but they're part of the presentation. Keeping those leaves on encourages people to notice that these turnips were freshly pulled from the ground by nimble fingers in the moonlight.

Carefully, we placed the turnips on the tile of the living room floor in front of a roaring fire. Che had the job of removing the old, yellow leaves from each turnip and leaving the good, green leaves. Noah and I were to sort the turnips by size. It didn't look good to bunch different-sized turnips together. That made the small ones look inferior. Instead, you put big ones together at five to a bunch. Smaller-sized ones went seven to a bunch, and the little babies were nine to a bunch. They tasted the same either way, but Mom insisted on a uniform presentation. So, my brothers and I sat there with twist ties, smelling the aroma of a casserole nearly ready to come out of the oven, and we bunched. After hours of effort, we had seven boxes of baby turnips, each box containing twenty-four bunches.

No other farmers in Yolo County were going to make their children sit on the floor and bunch turnips by size while they waited on their dinner. Nobody else was that crazy or desperate. That's how we got the orders from those little gourmet restaurants. But most of our sales, in those days, took place at the farmers' market, which was the only place I ever got my hands on actual cash.

Our "earn card" rate was significantly less than whatever the minimum wage was in the 1980s, but we didn't know that, and since Mom and Dad could have just ordered us to work for free, getting anything at all was pretty cool. We never saw much of that money, though. I remember using my first earn card, representing years' worth of work and valuing one hundred dollars, to open my first savings account, but other than that, the earn card money somehow never materialized.

Farmers' markets, however, were a whole different situation. My brothers and I knew the going rate for what everyone else got paid to work markets, and there was always cash on hand at the end of the day, so our parents had to pay us. I would horrify them by blowing my money on junk food when we stopped for gas at the *ampm* convenience store on the way home.

Once, I left the store with a heated frozen burrito, a Slurpee, candy bars, and chips, excited to devour it all. My dad looked at me with disgust and commented, "It's embarrassing to see you with all that junk." His comment changed nothing about the fact that my brothers and I were equally deprived of junk food and money, and therefore loved them both with a passion. Ironically, Dad's attempt to raise a batch of revolutionaries had instead put chips on our shoulders about never having any disposable income—a reality that pushed us all to embrace capitalism.

Sweet pea flowers were one of Mom and Dad's first cash crops. I'm sure it was Mom's idea to grow them, but Dad specialized in selling them at the markets. Every spring, those fragrant sweet pea flowers were our little farm's lifeline. In fact, Dad once grossed ten thousand dollars on an eighth of an acre of sweet peas. That was an unfathomable sum in those days, and it really made my parents believe in farming as a lifestyle and career.

I remember how gathering those sweet pea flowers was always a highlight of spring growing up. We would save tin cans from the kitchen all year long to use them as little vases for the bouquets of pea flowers. The box of mismatched cans told its own story about our diet: kidney beans, stewed tomatoes, black olives, cream of mushroom soup, garbanzo beans, pineapple, and the occasional dessert of peaches with syrup. We would arrange the sweet-pea-blossom-filled cans in boxes and pack those aromatic boxes into the van—fill it up to the brim.

The routine was to pick the flowers on a Friday afternoon and pack them into the reused tin cans filled with water. These got organized into reused tomato crates, which would sit on the porch overnight before they were loaded into the farmers'-market-bound blue van in the morning. One spring night, as freshly packed sweet pea flowers sat on the porch, my dad was awakened in the middle of the night by a commotion on the front porch. It was a skunk fighting with the cats, and it sprayed its musk all over the flowers! Not knowing what to do, Dad ran inside, grabbed the .22, and chased the critter down the dark driveway. The next morning, we worried about what the flowers would smell like at the market, but luckily nobody at the market said a word, and the flowers sold like hot cakes.

Sweet pea flower-selling days were the only times that the drive to the farmers' market didn't smell like composting produce, the typical smell of all our vehicles. The whole morning would be perfumed with these amazing flowers, and everyone would be in a good mood, no matter how little money we had or what scrapes and bruises we boys all suffered. Those sweet pea blossoms were the very scent of spring and better seasons ahead.

Mom used to talk about a story she wanted to publish in an amateur writing contest held by *Reader's Digest*. It was about one time when she was selling sweet pea flowers at the Marin Farmers' Market. California was in the midst of a drought, and everyone was talking about conserving water, which meant not flushing toilets when their contents were "yellow." A customer told Mom she liked to buy three bouquets and place them in the bathrooms in her house to fight the unpleasant odors.

"Get it?" the customer asked Mom pointedly: "Sweet pee!"

The success of sweet pea flowers led Mom and Dad to experiment with ambrosia melons, crimson sweet watermelons, thin-skinned potatoes, cherry tomatoes, mesclun lettuce, and other unique crops that became market favorites. Mom had an intuitive sense about what crops to grow, and Dad was the family expert at drawing in farmers' market customers in droves.

Dad liked to get a feel for which foods inspired people at the farmers' market each weekend. He knew customers were attracted to a certain energy and that energy came from the produce.

"Buy our produce!" Dad once shouted, "It's full of produce divas!"

"Don't you know?" he told passersby. "The further produce is driven from where it's grown, the more produce divas inside of it jump out! You don't want produce with no divas in it, do you? Buy from Capay

Fruits & Vegetables! Our produce has the best divas! It's powerful! It's addicting!"

Dad also knew that good salespeople were key to selling, and the best salespeople were attracted to the produce. Certain types would come to buy but would then just hang around, waiting for a job offer, so Dad used to offer them work in exchange for produce to see how they did. That's how our farm stand ended up with a good-looking gay man named Christopher, who would work the stand with his shirt off. Dad would tell one of his stories, like the one about the produce divas, and Christopher would stand there looking fascinated by his tale.

"Really?" Christopher would inquire. "Tell me more about the produce divas!"

People looking for good food flocked from near and far to enjoy Dad and Christopher's little show and to buy, buy, buy!

As a kid, my job at the markets was to facilitate the traffic flow through each of the recurring phases of the sales process. First, I cut samples and got my pitch ready. For our super-sweet Nantes carrots, I'd say: "Careful when you try these carrots. They're addicting!" For sweet snap peas: "Pop the top, peel the string, and eat the whole thing!" For Satsuma mandarins that ripened just before Christmas: "Santa-sumas! They make great stocking stuffers." Sungold cherry tomatoes prompted me to exclaim: "They look like tomatoes but taste like candy!"

Armed with samples and a pitch, I was ready to attract customers. Initially, there would always be rejection, though. Sometimes you can't even give product away, but such a drought would never last because eventually, someone would try it, word would spread, and pretty soon my one-line pitch would work wonders on passersby. Folks wouldn't be as nervous to try something new when people were already raving about it.

The small crowd that typically grew around my sample tray led to a lot of sales. So, I'd put the samples down, take the money, give them the goods, then go back to handing out samples. It never took long to work through a mounded-up plate of samples. By then, the stand would be picked through and need to be restocked. So, I'd restock the stand and fill the plate with even more samples. That was the routine:

restock, cut samples, give samples, take money, restock, cut samples, give samples, take money.

Dad instructed me that while giving out samples, I should tell people, "It's organic!" However, "organic" was not a household word back in the eighties, so I had to go on to explain that our produce was grown without synthetic pesticides or herbicides. That is, if people let me. Sometimes, they just shrugged at the unfamiliar term and walked on.

Once, when Che was working as the sample guy, a college professor at UC Davis strolled by. When Che said, "It's organic!" the professor just looked at Che funny and replied, "Son, we're *all* organic," meaning we're all composed of carbon and hydrogen. That was how unfamiliar the term was.

Although, as a little kid, I frequently explained the concept of "organic" to customers, I was just speaking the words I had been trained to say. I didn't know what it meant, since I had never seen a conventional farm up-close and didn't know there was any other type of farming but ours.

It wouldn't be until I was responsible for running the farm that I truly understood what "organic" meant, technically. Certified organic produce is food grown that follows a process that's verified annually by a third-party inspector who physically looks at each field and reviews the farm's documentation. Today, that standard is set by the National Organic Program, whose policy is governed by the United States Department of Agriculture and requires an annual third-party inspection.

In the early days of organics, there was no federal standard. In fact, the first organic standards were set by farmers who farmed organically and would simply inspect one another. The legal designation for organic produce came about when the California Organic Food Act of 1979 was signed into law. It legally defined organic practices but made no provisions for enforcement until 1990. Back then, we had a rubber stamp (which was pretty fancy office equipment for our farm). In bold black ink, it stamped: "Grown in accordance with the California Organic Foods Act of 1990" on every bill of lading that left the farm.

Broadly speaking, for a farm to be certified organic means that anything put onto an organic field must be naturally found on earth and not chemically altered from the form in which it was found. So, chicken manure mined from poultry operations is organic fertilizer, but natural gas mined from the earth, then mixed with nitrogen from the air at high temperatures and pressure in order to make ammonia—that is not an organic fertilizer. *Bacillus thuringiensis* (or Bt), which is a microbe naturally found in soil, can be grown and put onto plants to kill worms and is considered organic pesticide. However, genetically modifying plants to produce Bt in order to kill worms themselves is not considered organic.

Crushing plants to extract their oils, which are then sprayed onto other plants to deter bugs—that's considered an organic pesticide. But killing worms and other pests through methods like the esterification of phosphoric acid, oxidating phosphite esters, or using alcoholysis of phosphorus oxychloride to create organophosphates (which make up 50 percent of the killing agents in chemical pesticides)—this is not considered organic. In addition, genetically modified organisms (GMOs) are never permitted in organic farming. Fields must have been farmed under these conditions for three years before a field is certified organic. These rules encompass the vast majority of what it means to be certified organic.

Our organic certification aside, Capay Fruits & Vegetables really did have the most incredible produce around. People would taste those fresh, juicy melon samples and go wide-eyed, saying they had never tasted anything like that in their lives. Tomato samples at the peak of the season would bring some customers back to their childhood summers on a grandparent's farm. The smell of bouquets of sweet pea flowers used to bring back memories and even prompt tears from customers on the spot.

Sometimes, when fruit was peaking, and Dad got an especially good crowd, he would test the limits. For instance, one weekend, when the crimson sweet watermelons were at their best, he decided that every time he sold a watermelon, he would raise the price by a dollar and see how high he could go. He hawked his wares, gave out samples, and got a vibe going. A crowd of customers grew around the bin of melons. Soon, people bought melons as fast as Dad could take the money, and with each sale, he raised the price by a dollar. I was amazed when he got up to five, then six, then seven dollars apiece.

The samples acted like magic. People said they had never tasted anything like it. People walking by were drawn into the crowd, not wanting to miss out. They had to have a melon at any price! Eventually, Dad got up to where he charged one man twenty dollars for a watermelon.

The guy reached into his wallet, then stopped, looked at Dad, and asked, "Wait, *how* much?"

It was fun to watch Dad work the crowd. He had a way of creating a sense of mystery and scarcity around our produce. His claims were not far off the mark though, and his willingness to ask and even expect people to give him what he wanted was imperative to the success of our farmers' market adventures. There is a certain amount of showmanship to farmers' market sales, as well as a sense of being a puppet master making people go crazy for what you're selling. It's the kind of scene that can prompt people to pay twenty bucks for a single watermelon. I learned that from Dad.

By contrast, Mom's area of expertise came into play at the start of the growing season. She was expert in the art of selecting delicious, unusual varieties to grow, then harvesting them at the peak of ripeness. Dad was brilliant at drawing peoples' attention to Mom's success in this regard. Despite their differences, they were always a great team in that way, and my parents introduced some amazing fruits and vegetables into the market.

In the eighties, farmers' markets were the cutting edge of retail, providing venues for farms like ours to sell whatever we wanted. These were always early-morning events for which we had to get up way before the sun. Depending upon the season, there was always a mismatch of produce that had to fit into the van in those wee hours, but somehow, we had to get *all* of it in. Packing the truck was generally a two-person job that began with someone calling the job of "inside man." The others would then feed him boxes of produce. The inside man had the job of neatly organizing the boxes to ensure every cubic inch of space was utilized, but sometimes he had to be extra creative. For instance, if we had a lot of melons, the inside man would first request boxes of other produce, with which he would create a dam inside the van. Then, the "melon chain" would begin. We would line up and pass individual melons hand-over-hand until they reached the inside man, who corralled them in the space created by the dam of produce boxes. Loading market vans taught me a life skill that I still appreciate to this day—I always get everything to fit.

These markets were the only thing that consistently got us boys off the farm and enabled us to say we had been to the big city of San Francisco. In addition, they served as a proving ground where us kids became quite comfortable in the presence of adults. Perhaps most importantly, we realized at the markets that there actually was a demand for the fruits and vegetables our farm produced. You see, my brothers and I only had eyes for processed food. Personally, we viewed cabbage, carrots, bok choy, and such as utterly worthless.

I remember how I used to humbly take a bag filled with substandard vegetables—indeed, they were going to be fed to the chickens when we got home—and successfully trade them with a baker at the farmers' market for a sweet sticky bun. Each time I did it, I would cringe, expecting him to say, "No way, kid!" Miraculously, though, I walked away each time with a treat.

Unfortunately, word about my little scheme got out to my brothers. The golden goose I had found was soon killed when all four of us approached the baker at once, and he protested: "I don't need any more kale!"

Naturally, this confirmed our suspicion that vegetables were of limited value.

Besides bread and brown rice, though, vegetables comprised a large part of our diet. The farm occasionally produced hogs as well as eggs and chickens, but overall, our diets were light on protein. Our attempts to raise chickens, in particular, were downright comical.

Just like on old-fashioned, turn-of-the-century farms, whatever we didn't sell or can for the winter became scraps we put to use as chicken feed. As such, dumping kitchen compost into the chicken coop was a routine household chore for us kids. We would then collect, wash, and pack the eggs for the weekend's markets. However, we had one mean, gray hen who viciously defended her nest of eggs.

You could push most hens aside before gently taking the warm eggs from beneath them, but not with the gray. Sticking your hand into her nest box would earn you a pecking that drew blood. So, we developed a technique where you could pin the gray hen into a corner with a stick and steal her eggs with your free hand. We also had a rooster who loved to attack small children. He once penned me into a corner. When I made a break for it, I tripped and fell, and he took full advantage of the situation by pecking at my head while I struggled and screamed. When I later ran to my mother, bloodied, she resolved to clean house on that worthless chicken coop once and for all. Egg production was declining anyway. (That rooster may have gotten the last laugh, though, because when I fell that day, I split open my forehead and still have a nice scar to show for it to this day.) By the time of the rooster attack, Dad was already actively culling the less productive hens in order to make the chicken feed go further, so he added the rooster to his list.

However, on our farm, we never had the right tool for anything. This was never truer than with the killing of poultry.

The right way to harvest a chicken is with a special, flexible, plastic cone. You put it over the chicken so just its head sticks out. Someone then holds the cone down on a surface, which suppresses the chicken's ability to flap for freedom. With the neck pulled taught over the end of a log, one swipe from an ax cuts the chicken's head off, and it bleeds out while the body twitches, trapped inside the cone. Dad had acquired one of those cones from a friend at the market, but it was a big one for turkeys. So, when he resolved to turn that rooster into dinner, Dad put it in the cone and cut the head off, but the rooster's body slipped out of the cone and flapped around wildly without its head, blood spurting everywhere—all over the cone, the rooster, and all of us standing there, until finally the bird ran out of blood and fell lifeless on the ground. We kids watched this scene absolutely agog. For the rest of our lives, we would have a very clear visual to follow the phrase, "running around like a chicken with its head cut off." That is a thing that really happens.

After that disaster, Dad sought a different method to dispose of the nonproductive chickens. We loaded the old hens into produce boxes, put them into the blue van, and drove them to the rolling hills behind my grandparents' house, which were used for running sheep. There, beside the dirt road, we found a beautiful, scenic spot and set the old chickens free. We knew they would be eaten by coyotes, but at least they'd die on their own terms, feisty as ever. That's how a piece of land we called Chicken Heaven got its name.

Raising pigs was, for the most part, an equally unprofitable venture. I raised a few for 4-H but always found it difficult to buy enough feed when we were in town. We never had enough money to buy much, and we never knew when the next trip to town would be, so we often ran out of pig feed. I remember one pig in particular. For some reason, I kept it longer than usual and it would mow through feed so quickly that often it would have to wait days to eat until our next trip to town. I used to lose sleep thinking about my poor pig with no food. Sometimes, it would escape from its pen to forage around the farm, which I didn't mind because it eased my stress about the situation. So, when we finally had the money and time and got organized enough to call the mobile slaughter guy whose job it was to slaughter and process the pig, I wasn't the least bit sentimental. I was, in fact, relieved to have the stress of caring for that pig out of my life.

Animal husbandry was a skill we simply never mastered at Capay Fruits & Vegetables, so our diets were highly vegetable-and-grain based, to the point where, one day, on the way home from the farmers' market, a tired, ten-year-old Che sprawled in the back of the van and, in a faint but forceful voice, bellowed, "I neeeeeeed meat!"

The poor kid was starving for protein. Mom felt so bad about it that she stopped at the market and bought ground beef for hamburgers that night. There was a limit, after all, to her idealism.

Part of the secret to our success with fruit was the small size of our farm and the fact that what we picked didn't have to last long. Our produce would literally be picked, sold, and eaten within a couple of days, if not the very next day. Because of this, we could grow varieties with a lot of sugar and harvest them at their peak ripeness. The more sugar in a fruit or vegetable, the more easily it breaks and bruises, so such produce can't be shipped far or stored long.

Big farms, with their national markets and long distribution systems, didn't grow these varieties because the fruit just didn't last long enough to look good by the time the customer got them. The same thing is still true today. That's why, in most supermarkets, you don't get the super-sweet carrots or figs picked at their peak ripeness. America's mainstream food system incentivizes farms to produce varieties that yield high, ship well, and look good, while minimizing the production cost per unit, with little or no regard for flavor. That's the food most folks are used to, and it's why our farm's produce sometimes really used to blow peoples' minds . . . and still does.

The second key to our success, such as it was, was the way we selected the best varieties. When consumers buy local produce, it's not just better for the environment or safer for them, it's better produce, because small, local farms can grow sweeter varieties, pick them at their peak ripeness, and sell them directly to people who will eat them within days. Better yet, the CSA program, Farm Fresh To You, which Mom would start in 1993, enabled us to deliver this ultra-fresh produce directly to the consumer without even the delay of waiting for a market day.

I remember, once, when we had enjoyed yet another one of those incredible weekends at the farmers' market where Dad sold everything at top dollar to enthusiastic buyers, we were really on a roll. Every weekend that season had been good, four-figure days. On the drive home, we all cheered and laughed, happy in our empty van, celebrating a rare week of financial solvency. There was a feeling in the air that maybe things were turning around for Capay Fruits & Vegetables. In fact, *Newsweek* had recently run an article about us, featuring an adorable photo of Mom and Dad washing vegetables while an orange cat looked on, appearing to inspect their work. I didn't realize at the time what a big deal it was for us to be in *Newsweek*, but in hindsight, the article was proof that we really were on the cutting edge of a movement.

Yet, on Monday, when Mom sat down to pay bills, she couldn't figure out why we didn't have enough money. Finally, with furrowed brow, she said, "Martin, this isn't enough to pay the bills! I don't get it. We've done so well this month!" I had seen her in this distressed state many times, doing and redoing calculations on paper, trying to figure out how to keep the lights on, somehow.

Dad smiled mischievously, ran upstairs, and returned a moment later, looking triumphant and proffering a stack of hundred-dollar bills. Apparently, for months, he had been keeping all the hundreds we earned at the farmers' market in his sock drawer so he could "come to the rescue" on a day like this. My brothers and I were just excited to see the stack of hundreds. We had no idea how messed up it was that Dad had created a crisis in order to be a hero, but Mom was no fool.

Around that time, whatever Mom had originally loved and admired about Martin started wearing off. Ten plus years into the marriage, with four boys, she now needed a partner to work with her to raise a family and achieve financial solvency, but Dad was still the same man he had been as a college student. He still passionately questioned the status quo, but along with that came a habit of doing whatever he wanted with no care for consequences.

Our family television lived on a rolling cart that was normally tucked into a closet under the stairs. Rolling it out, plugging it in, and adjusting the bunny ears until we got a signal was often a lot more trouble than it was worth, and, anyway, we weren't allowed to fool with it when the sun was shining. By design, the lack of television in our lives forced us to make up our own games and concoct ever-more-elaborate ideas for adventures. Che once invented a sail to power a bicycle. We made a game of jumping off the roof of a shed and climbed the eucalyptus trees that bordered our twenty acres. We also taunted our cantankerous neighbor Johnny and fought one another incessantly. There were no rules, just the knowledge that Mom had no time to drive any of her wild brood to the hospital.

Once, Noah collapsed in the driveway, totally dehydrated, after riding his bike home from school in excruciating heat. Mom, who was watering a garden at the time, simply walked over and watered her son like a plant. It worked! Another time, I broke my thumb in a horse accident and Mom made a splint for it with popsicle sticks and tape. That didn't work. I ended up driving myself to the hospital but only after spending the weekend deer hunting with that nasty thumb. When the doctor saw the X-ray, he chuckled and said, "Whoa! That's a spectacular break! Don't eat anything today. You'll be in for surgery in the morning."

On our way back from the surgery, we stopped to get gas. The convenience store had an ICEE machine, with its sweet, frozen, chemical-packed goodness in a cup. I asked Mom if I could have one.

"Thaddeus, those things are terrible for you!" she lectured. "They're filled with so many chemicals. You shouldn't put that stuff in your body." But Mom saw I wasn't deterred by these facts, so she yielded and said, "Okay, you can have one if you promise me you'll never eat another one as long as you live!"

I responded, "Deal!"

To this day, I think of my mother every time I have a slushie.

In those days, things between us boys got violent quickly. The way I remember it, Noah was the catalyst. For instance, when I was about six, Che tried to teach me how to defend myself against his twin. In the house, we had a rack for organizing magazines, which held a dozen

or so long, straight pieces of wood to which you could attach magazines. When it was being used, *Newsweek*, *Time*, and *National Geo-
graphic* dangled neatly from clips on those sticks. However, the rack
was seldom used for that. Instead, we used the sticks as swords and
drumsticks. One day, after Noah and I had had a blow-up, Che saw an
opportunity to give his little brother some advice.

He grabbed one of those sticks, took me aside, and gave me a pep
talk. Che told me the next time Noah came at me, I should beat him
with the magazine stick. As he spoke, he demonstrated by clenching
the stick fiercely and taking swings at an imaginary opponent. He ended his pep talk with advice: "If you beat Noah with that stick, he'll
never mess with you again."

I was inspired and believed that with this knowledge and weapon
I could level our seven-year gap and finally beat the shit out of Noah.

Sure enough, one day, Noah came for me. I wielded the weapon
and, for a split second, saw the fear in Noah's eyes as he contemplated
what was about to happen. That detail made me hesitate, though. In
reality, I didn't have the hate in me needed to really try to harm him, so
Noah seized the stick from me. I thought, *Shit, I'm done for*, and braced
for a beating. Noah didn't beat me, though.

Being the third child in the family, I had to demand whatever attention I got, and I imagine this drove my older brothers, particularly
Noah, crazy. So, there were other violent incidents that, in fairness to
Noah, I likely deserved. I have vivid memories of being water-board-
ed outside the house in the stock tank that served as the pool. Once,
upstairs in the house, Noah pinned my biceps to the ground with his
knees, took my hands, and forced me to hit myself in the face with
them. There was only one thing I could do, so I did it: I spat a huge
loogy onto his face. He was disgusted, and for a moment I thought I
had won. Then, he reciprocated.

Those were the *Lord of the Flies* years. Alone with each other after
school, things got way out of hand, but we didn't know what was normal. We were just being ourselves. Somehow, though, we boys not only
survived our childhoods but bonded through it all. It was probably
the isolation that did it. We lived our lives as if stranded together on

a deserted island, out there on the farm. Any type of civilization was an hour-long bike ride away. When we got bored, we used to come up with ever-wilder bicycle stunts that would have sent normal kids to the hospital, but not us.

One time, Che wiped out so badly that I ran inside to tell Mom but couldn't get out the words because of a stutter I had. In a panic, I acted out Che's entire bicycle stunt and the way he had landed in a heap, melded with both the broken bike and the red wagon he had attempted to jump over. Although my voice was silenced by the stutter, my fingers described the rivulets of blood cascading over Che's face. Mom watched all this in a state of high concentration, then sprang into action with her first-aid kit.

At some point in the early eighties, when the twins were about nine or ten, Noah, Che, and Mom were flying somewhere in an airplane. As the plane glided over the land, my brothers looked out the window at big circles in the green cropland below.

"What are those circles?" Che asked Mom.

"That's a center-pivot irrigation system," Mom explained.

Center-pivot irrigation involves a horizontal, overhead irrigation pipe attached to a vertical pipe coming out of a water source in the middle of a field. The pipe rotates around the center pivot, spraying water in a circle from sprinkler heads on the revolving bar. It's a totally automated system.

When Che saw how easy an automated irrigation could be, he just sat there wide-eyed, realizing for the first time that there are farmers in the world who do not move irrigation pipe from one side of the field to the other every day. By extension, he realized there are farmers with big machines to do things for them who don't use their children as farmhands. From an early age, Che hated inefficiency, and realizations like this drove him harder toward his dream of flying up above it all as a pilot.

One day, after Mom and four-year-old Freeman gave some of the farm crew a ride home, my innocent little brother made an observation about all the things we transported in the van.

"Mom," he said, "you know how different flowers smell different? People smell different too. We have our own smell, and the farm workers have their own smell."

Mom was a bit dumbfounded by her preschooler's observation. While one could consider it rude to talk about how people smell, the kid was right. Who could blame him for noticing?

"It's true," she replied. "Different people smell different ways, and that's okay!"

Freeman's observation brought to light an important fact about our lifestyle on the farm: despite our relative seclusion in Capay Valley, we were exposed to many cultures and lifestyles, more so, I think, than average country kids. Capay Valley was a tiny patch in the middle of a Venn diagram where numerous circles of American culture overlapped. There were your educated, back-to-the-land hippies. Then you had blue-collar, Caucasian families and a few Black kids. Add to that the mostly Mexican farm workers, some of whom were our employees—some migrant, some not; some with green cards, some not. And don't forget the local "Indian" tribe, then called the Rumsey Indian Rancheria, a few miles up the highway from our farm. (Now they're called the Yocha Dehe Wintun Nation, or simply "The Tribe.") There were Japanese Americans, too, as some of the families that were moved to internment camps during World War II had had the fortitude to return and buy back the land that was stolen from them. Our living in this confluence of cultures was no accident. In fact, one of the few things my parents always agreed on was that they weren't going to raise their children in an insular, middle class, American echo chamber like the suburbs where they had both grown up.

For kids in this community, the school bus was the great equalizer. All these different types of families put their children on the same yellow number seven school bus, and no matter what we had or did not have, we were stuck waiting at the ends of our driveways for the same bus in the same heat and cold and rain and snow. We rode back on it together, too, all of us equally impatient to get home at the end of a long day. My brothers and I navigated this world by getting along with everyone while having just one or two close friends apiece.

Our parents were pleased to see us tossed into this cultural mix. However, they had no idea how truly ignorant we were about our neighbors. After all, culture and race simply weren't discussed much out in the sticks. For instance, I didn't understand that the "Indian" kids at school were Native Americans. Since they were brown and didn't speak Spanish, I thought they were the kind of Latinos that had lived in California so long they didn't speak Spanish anymore. Then, one day, when I was eight years old, we got the day off school for Martin Luther King, Jr.'s birthday, and I was confronted with my ignorance head-on. My friend Alfonso came to the farm for the day off and we walked around while Pup, my family's black lab mutt, trotted alongside. We discussed why we had the day off school, and Alfonso spoke ill of Martin Luther King, Jr. I was shocked at his ignorance and used the opportunity to show off my own.

"How can you not like Martin Luther King, Jr.?" I asked. "If it weren't for him, you wouldn't be free!"

Alfonso's eyes popped out of his head as he exclaimed, "I am not Black!"

He ran over to the dog and held his arm against the black fur on Pup's body, saying, "That is black! I am brown! You see the difference?"

My White ass blushed red with embarrassment. As an eight-year-old, I genuinely believed Martin Luther King, Jr. was responsible for the emancipation of the slaves. I knew nothing about the civil rights movement of the 1960s. What's more, in my ignorance, I saw only White people and non-White people. My friend's reaction was what prompted me to try get this information sorted out.

Eventually, in college, a history instructor put it to my class plainly, stating: "It is a fact that the United States of America is based on the complete destruction of another people."

The patriotic American in me bristled and didn't want to believe this about my country, but as a child, I had seen it myself—the way nearly everyone in the community tried to push the Indians back down into generational poverty, as if they didn't have a right to thrive like the rest of us.

During the eighties, the federal Indian Gaming Regulatory Act empowered the Rumsey Indian Rancheria to open a bingo hall in a small, humble, metal building just up the road from us. After that, the highway that ran by our farm, generally so devoid of traffic it was sometimes used to herd sheep, was no longer empty all the time. On a set schedule, bingo would let out, and a long, steady stream of traffic flowed down the road, which raised the ire of local farmers.

Sadly, a bingo hall customer ran over and killed our farm dog, Pup. I blamed the bingo parlor and told Mom how some of the kids at school said it was "invading" our rural lifestyle. Sad as she was about Pup, Mom couldn't suppress a sardonic laugh. She reminded me that we, too, were "invaders" in a land where we didn't originate. And so, too, were those complaining farmers.

"Who was here before Johnny and Gale and Cliff and all of them?" she asked.

I had never thought about it.

"The Indians," she said. "So, who's invading whom?"

Mom didn't talk much about social and political topics like these, but generally speaking, she made my brothers and me understand that morals were important, evil was a presence that stalked the earth, and integrity was not lost all at once, but a little bit at a time. Whenever I tried on the coat of bigotry that was easy to pick up at school, Mom was the one who ripped it off and helped me see the line between right and wrong.

Very few non-Indians saw it Mom's way, and everyone from farmers to businessmen to politicians voiced outrage about the bingo parlor. You would hear guys talking at the gas station, saying they were going to put a tractor with a flat tire in the middle of the road to cause havoc with the bingo traffic, stuff like that. Well, they never did beat The Tribe, and that little bingo parlor eventually turned into the wildly successful Cache Creek Casino Resort, which now invests hundreds of millions of dollars into the local economy. Mom stayed out of the public conversation about this issue, but I know she would have cheered to see them succeed.

Years later, as an adult, I rekindled a friendship with a guy from The Tribe who I had grown up with, which really enabled me to open my eyes to his point of view about his people and their history. I wish my family and community had been more open-minded about acknowledging their point of view, the reality of the tragedy they suffered, and their experience being on the receiving end of colonialism. With this understanding, perhaps we could have been more excited for their opportunity to run a bingo parlor. Certainly, any family in the Capay Valley would have been excited to run a lucrative business like that bingo parlor on behalf of their family.

Not having sisters definitely made it tough for us boys to learn anything about girls, but we grew up to be genuine feminists, and no mistake. We knew women to be as strong and able as men in every way. In our family, it was our mother's voice that rang with authority. She was the level-headed and steadfast parent who was always there for us and had our best interests at heart. Sometimes that meant breaking a wooden spoon over our asses or washing our mouths out with soap, but just as fiercely as she ran the house, she loved us.

Knowing this, I remember finding it strange that when I used to tag along on errands around town, it was Dad to whom people were helpful and kind, not Mom. At the local equipment dealership, the technicians condescended to Mom and assumed she didn't know what part she really needed for her tractor. They made sexist cracks right to her face, but for Dad they bent over backward. It's a good thing they were extra helpful to him, too, because he had no idea what he was doing. Mom was the brains of the operation, and we boys knew it, even if others denied this obvious truth.

We had friends, though—people who knew our reality. One time a local guy was visiting the farm and saw my mother walking with her head down, dejected by the toil of the farm. He called out, "Kathy, you walk with your head high!" It touched my heart to see Mom get a fraction of the recognition she deserved.

Naturally, though, among us kids on the number seven bus, the Indians, the migrant workers' kids, the Latinos, the conventional farmers' kids, the hippie farm kids, and my brothers and I (whatever we were), we were far more concerned with escaping bullies, flirting with one another, and experimenting with a cigarette or sip of beer in the way-back than with whatever adult issues concerned our parents. Meanwhile, Freddie, the bus driver, was too busy looking for deer to notice any of it. Although, on occasion, we got loud enough that he would pull the bus over, walk down the aisle and yell at all of us equally, maybe even twist an ear or two.

Overall, my brothers and I gravitated toward the hardest working, most friendly, and most innately clever people in our school who ranged across the cultural mix. Our childhood gave us a background where it was natural to see the world through the eyes of many different people, regardless of the color of their skin, their gender, or any other assigned classification. Of all the lessons we learned as children, this is the one of which I am most appreciative.

Chapter Five
·SEPTEMBER 2000·

The sudden, alarming *tch-tch-tch* of a Northern Pacific Rattlesnake sounds deep and fast and unnatural. No human could shake a rattle as fast as that snake shakes its tail. It does so as a courtesy. After all, the snake does not want to waste valuable energy biting you, and you don't want to deal with the pain of being bit, so learning to respect this warning is a win-win for everyone. It can be difficult, though, to arrest your forward momentum the instant you hear the rattle, before the snake feels so threatened it must sink its fangs into your unprotected ankle or calf. This sound is not one people are born to fear, like a snarling dog, but something learned. Yet, once you've been face-to-face with an angry rattlesnake, even once, you respect that sound the next time you hear it.

In early September of 2000, just a few months after Mom left us, I inspected the pepper crop. We had five different varieties of sweet peppers as well as red and yellow bell peppers. Mom had planted these back in April, thank goodness, so there was not much I could do to screw them up, and they thrived all season. The tops of the plants showed small white flowers above tiny, mature peppers, too small to sell. The plants, now nearing the end of their life cycle, had served us well.

Mom couldn't afford all the drip irrigation equipment she would have liked to buy, but (as compared to the movable irrigation pipes) this pressurized system of tiny hoses that slowly drips water into the earth at a steady rate is a highly efficient way to irrigate crops without wasting water through evaporation, runoff, or watering unwanted weeds, so this year she had dedicated the drip system to this pepper field. The results paid off.

Although pepper plants thrive in summer heat, they're easily burned by the sun. The trick is to plant them early enough that they grow big leaves before they start fruiting, so the little peppers are shaded through the productive summer months. That year, not only were the peppers fat and healthy and free of sunburn, but the field had stayed clean of weeds. I could see where the soil between the plants stayed dark from a steady stream of pressurized water. I was glad we had at least done this one thing right.

I walked through the field, appreciating these details, when suddenly the unmistakable hiss of a rattlesnake's warning jolted me into panic. Without thought, I sprang into the air shrieking a four-letter word and landed right in the middle of a patch of peppers the next row over. I gathered my limbs about me and crouched, eyes peeled for the serpent that was surely readying to end my life. Finally, I spied the source of the rattle: a hissing orifice on the drip hose. It sputtered out one last bubble of pressurized air.

Embarrassed, I looked around to see who in the field was bound to taunt me the rest of my natural life for shrieking in fear of an irrigation hose. Nobody was around, though. I was equal parts relieved and disappointed. After all, the funny scene would have been memorable, for sure.

Not with any malice toward the hose in question, my next act would be to remove the irrigation from this field. Along with eggplant, basil, and okra, peppers yielded their final marketable fruit in September and would soon have to be disked back into the ground as we prepared the field for winter. This preparation feels like a violent act. A tractor pulls a flail mower over the beautiful, two-foot-high pepper plants. It shreds them and their stubby final fruits into pieces until the whole field looks like a sea of green with the plants' resilient little stubs sticking up all over. The smell is exquisite—so sweet, so alive, as if the life essence from the now-dead plants has suffused the air and entered your lungs for one last hurrah of existence.

Next, if the ground needs it, we spread truckloads of minerals or compost, and finally a tractor will disk the stubs, mulch, compost, and minerals into the soil like one big blender, making a nutritious earth smoothie to nourish next year's crop. All this churning displaces insects from their burrows, inviting flocks of wild turkeys to waddle in from the hedgerows to feast on the insects. Then, before the fall rains, we plant a legume cover crop mix, which is the cornerstone of our farm's sustainability. This crop stops weeds from growing, protects the soil from erosion in the winter, fixes organic nitrogen into the soil, and builds organic matter. By comparison, less sustainable farms will clean their fields and keep them bare as scorched earth, not letting anything grow on or in the soil until they're ready to plant their next crop.

In September of 2000, we still rented a field from old man Gale—that neighbor in a wheelchair who was always feuding with Johnny and Cliff. We liked the field and knew exactly what would thrive there in each season. It was familiar territory, which is a prerequisite to success. Trouble was, Gale was as particular about his fields as an aircraft mechanic with his tools.

He didn't want any fiddleneck growing anywhere. The puncture vine had to be pulled up just as the flowers turned yellow. He didn't want anyone to drive too fast and kick up dust. He wanted the driveway graveled at the end of every year. He didn't want the farm workers he derisively called "The Mexicans" on the field at all. The list of his demands was endless and utterly impossible to fulfill.

Mom used to have a special way with Gale. She was like a snake charmer getting that vicious cobra right back down into his basket. Gale, who seemed to like nobody, had liked Mom, but not so much our new farm manager Chris. So, as the growing season really got underway, Chris's phone rang off the hook with late-night, complaint-filled calls from Gale.

Before I returned to college, I resolved to try to help Chris develop some kind of working relationship with Gale. So, one day, he and I arrived at Gale's house for an agreed-upon meeting. Gale met us at the door looking just like the old man I remembered from childhood, only older, with his wheelchair, gray flat-top, five-day beard, crooked teeth, and crooked jaw to match. His shaking, palsied, claw-shaped hands clutched the wheelchair arms, and fuzzy bunny slippers adorned feet at the end of legs so thin it was obvious they hadn't moved in decades.

Immediately, Gale lit into the subject of "The Mexicans." He thought they were stealing his tools left, right, and center. He claimed they had sped past his house that very day and dusted his laundry on the line. He even sent his wife out into the yard to bring back a specimen of his dusty drawers as evidence. He further claimed that while she was out there, one of The Mexicans flirted with her.

This term, "The Mexicans," always offended me, as if saying someone had roots in a particular place was an insult. After all, everyone comes from somewhere. Many of our crew were indeed Mexican American, but one time (long before this) I had pointed out that many of them were from Nicaragua, Guatemala, and Peru, but poor Gale thought those were all places in Mexico. I found such profound ignorance in a grown man both funny and tragic, but it definitely stopped me from trying to reason with him further. Our employees were harder working human beings than everyone who ever insulted them, but I could not really stand up for them the way I wanted to at that particular meeting, as we desperately needed to farm the old man's land.

Furthermore, Gale had opinions about our irrigation processes, which really were not his business, but he made them his business. We had to use his pump, which was included in the lease, to get the water, and he had something to say about that, too, as if there were more than one way to use a pump. You turn it on. You turn it off. Who could complain about that? But Gale did. He could complain about a dust mote dancing in a sunbeam, that guy. There was nothing on this earth Gale could not find some way to complain about.

I had set up this meeting under the naive assumption that if we simply spoke reasonably to the man, we could all come to some agreement. No way. Gale did not want anything so much as to be a pain in everyone's ass. I think he had nothing going on in his life other than pointing out everyone else's errors. He did not even appreciate people who were trying to appease him, except insofar as they could function as targets for his rage. Gale even accused Chris and me of growing marijuana on our farm (in 2000 that was still illegal). In fact, Gale was so nuts, he told us a helicopter had supposedly raided his house the very night before, looking for our weed. Chris and I could barely hold back our laughter as we wondered what kind of bad trip Gale's prescription meds had put him through the night before. By the end of what Chris and I had intended to be a reasonable, neighborly meeting, we felt like our brains were exploding, or maybe Gale's was. His face had turned red with all the ranting and raving.

In truth, our meeting that year probably made things worse between Chris and Gale. I resolved never to try to "talk sense" with the old man again and realized then and there that the best way to deal with a character like that is to give him as little attention as possible. We could not ignore Gale entirely, or he would go crazy and seek revenge. Instead, we had to spoon-feed him just enough appeasement to keep him at arm's length, otherwise his urge to micromanage would consume us. I am sure Mom learned that lesson, too, long ago, but in this, as in so many things, I had to start from scratch and relearn it all.

When I got back to the farm, I told Ricardo about my ill-fated attempt to reason with Gale. He had known the old man as long as Mom and I had. Being Mexican, Ricardo took the brunt of the old man's ire on a regular basis, but he just laughed it off. Ricardo—so essential to the operation of this farm—had long ago mastered the art of humility to a degree I may never achieve.

Walking around the farm that September of 2000, I wandered past several fields, then stopped and considered the fig orchard. I did not like the looks of it. Many leaves were turning yellow and falling to the ground. The trees, in fact, looked like they were dying. I found Ricardo and suggested he water the figs more. He did not seem to like the idea but said okay.

Next, I watched with pleasure as leeks, kale, chard, lettuce, fennel, and beets were cultivated. Planting each of those crops in neat lines down the bed meant we could run a metal blade just under the soil in the places where the plants were not, thus killing most of the weeds. After the tractor finished planting, a hoeing crew was tasked with removing the rest of the weeds by hand. This combination of prevention and hand-weeding is the only way to keep organic fields weed free. The hundreds of man-hours of this labor-intensive work is not fun to pay for, but it is fun to watch. The field where weeds fought the crops for resources looked unkempt, but as workers moved down the rows, that chaos fell away and strips of brown earth dotted with evenly spaced plants replaced it. That particular day, this colorful scene was enhanced by the sight of Esparto Unified School District's, bright yellow, number seven Capay Valley school bus passing through the background on Highway 16.

September is a transitional time—not just for school children, but for farms too. For a lot of vegetables, summer harvest ends, but the winter squash and fall vegetables will not be ready to harvest until October. Many of Mom's fieldworkers used to leave in the fall when work slowed down. It meant a trip back to Mexico or Central America for a nice, warm winter spent with family. The next planting season, the undocumented among these migrant workers would have to get themselves smuggled back into California via "coyotes," but the risk and expense must have been worth it, because this is how they, our farm, and American agriculture in general kept body and soul together for decades, all facilitated by a relatively porous border.

Today, the border is guarded much more vigilantly than it used to be, so this style of migrant labor has largely stopped, ending the era when masses of migrant farm workers were available on an as-needed basis. Ironically, produce from Mexico (where workers are paid a few dollars a day and protected by no labor laws) flows across that same boarder breezily. That is a topic I could go into forever, but it's a story for another day.

Now, in order to keep help on hand for the busy summer season, farms need to either hire year-round documented workers or get really good at utilizing guest worker programs, which means a lot of time spent filling out paperwork. That also means farms—small, large, conventional, and organic, all of them—must now focus on getting more done with machines and be very organized about planning for the labor needed for the seasons when they need it. The way we manage these needs on our farm today is to focus on always having something for our core crew to do, year-round, which often means growing things we know we are going to lose money on. But overall, those losing crops contribute revenue toward keeping our essential, stable, year-round crew. There are also advantages to year-round help. For instance, that September we had a lot more workers than before to do the field prep work, and I was grateful for all the help I could get.

There are a lot of great advantages to small farms. They enable people to eat locally, visit the source of their food, and put better nutrition and taste into their diet. Small farms also build a stronger local economy, but cost savings is not among their advantages. The economic reality of small, organic farms is that they are expensive to run, which, for Mom, created even more reliance on her CSA subscription customers, whose memberships gave her a steady income stream that evened out the ups and downs of the seasons.

Disking green-waste compost into the fields helps keep them fertile, but weeds like fertile soil, too, and they can overwhelm and choke out the crop. This is especially true for carrots, so we use a system called solarization to kill weed seeds without herbicides in our carrot fields. Like a lot of organic farming techniques, solarizing requires preparing the field far ahead of time so it can be ready to plant in September. Once a field is mulched and composted and ready to plant, we wet it down with sprinklers, then roll a thin layer of clear plastic over the seed beds. This must be done by the end of May, so that when it gets really hot in June and July, the sun bakes the soil inside that plastic, raising the temperature to as high as one hundred and forty degrees, which kills many of the weed seeds lurking in the top few inches of the soil.

At this point, the soil is still dense with nutrients, but all the weed seeds are dead, so it is ready for whatever we want to plant. In September, we remove the plastic and plant carrots in the solarized fields. If all goes well, there will be no hand-weeding needed at all, but even in the worst-case scenario, the weeding bill is noticeably smaller than it would have been without solarizing. Luckily for me, before Mom died, Terry had already put the plastic down for her, right on schedule, so all I had to do was reap the rewards of their excellent preparation.

That September, Freeman and I lived in a room in the barn with our friend Danny. Since he was looking for work, and we were short on delivery drivers, we set Danny up to help with farmers' markets and produce deliveries. At that time, our field crews were still harvesting heirloom tomatoes like crazy. Our wholesale buyer was willing to take all we had, so the only problem was not having a truck big enough to transport the lot. Where there's a will, there's a way, though, so Danny and I hatched a plan.

After filling the normal delivery van with tomatoes, I hooked up the horse trailer to the truck and filled it with tomatoes too. All this occurred after a full day of working the farmers' market, so we were exhausted, but ripe tomatoes wait for no one. When Danny and I showed up that evening at the produce dock in San Francisco, dog tired, the workers on the docks just loved that we had improvised a horse trailer as a tomato truck and cheered this incredibly clever way of dealing with shipping issues. We had to laugh when they all whooped and hollered with enthusiasm. We had, after all, brought in a ridiculous amount of tomatoes, and the wholesaler had buyers for all of them. Basically, we broke up the dock workers' boring day with our out-of-the-box thinking. The folks from the upstairs office even came down to take pictures!

This story makes me laugh today because it took place well before the new focus on food safety. Food safety standards now dominate the produce business, so if I tried to deliver tomatoes in a horse trailer today, the entire shipment of produce would be rejected, and I'd be expected to dispose of all of it because of potential exposure to animal feces.

When Danny and I finally returned to the farm after that grueling day, I was ready to drop, but strangely, Danny had quite a bit of pep in his step. When I crashed into the bed, he stayed up and cleaned the room with manic energy.

"What are you doing?" I grumbled.

"I think I took too many of those Yellow Jacket energy pills!" he said. "I was tired when we got gas, so I bought them at the gas station. The package said to take two, but I took six!"

"Good luck with that," I mumbled and went to sleep.

The next morning, understandably, Danny was in terrible shape.

A year later, the FDA made that pill, ephedra, illegal. That is when I realized how dangerous what Danny had done was. We got that crop to market, though, which might have been solely thanks to those Yellow Jackets. In the fall of 2000, when I was afraid of losing the farm just about every day, selling tomatoes was the only thing that mattered. To hell with our health, safety, or well-being. I basically did not even have time to be human.

Weeks after I first asked Ricardo to water the figs, I noticed the failing fig orchard again and was not pleased. Again, I sought out Ricardo where he worked in the carrot field and asked him to double up the water on the figs. Did he not see they were dying? Why, I wondered, was I the only one to notice this? Those fig trees were as old as me, and I worried incessantly that in my first few months of running the family farm I had somehow managed to kill them.

I walked back to the house and visited Mom's tree. Somewhere inside, I think I expected it to grow miraculously from her ashes, a testament to the fact that her soul was thriving in heaven or something. But no, Mom's purple locust looked positively sickly. In fact, it looked dead. My heart broke to see that.

As dusk took hold of the farm, I sat on the engraved rock that served as Mom's tombstone, looked at my hands where the skin still peeled off in layers (I had gotten used to it), and contemplated the death of her tree. Starlings flitted in and out of trees nearby, but not Mom's tree. They wanted nothing to do with it.

Starlings are a bird about which I have mixed feelings. Their little arrow-shaped bodies are beautiful to watch, and the way their flocks dip and sway in total synchrony, like schools of fish, is fascinating, almost miraculous. In fact, as the evening light changes, the colors of the starling flocks seem to change too. Sunset colors reflect off the birds' iridescent wings and shine through the slender spaces between each bird in their dense clouds.

Sadly, starlings are also gourmands and invasive, with an excellent appreciation for the farm-to-table organic lifestyle we promote here but without the means to pay their share. They settle into the most perfectly ripe fig and peach orchards and chow down, poking holes in everything and making the entire crop unfit for human consumption.

In our youth, to protect our livelihood, Freeman and I spent many hours trying to hunt the elusive starlings, but they outsmarted us every time. We even set up a "bird cannon" designed to make the starlings think someone with a shotgun was protecting the grapes all day and night. It took exactly twenty-four hours for the starlings to recognize the scam. In fact, I would go so far as to say a flock of starlings can visually discern the difference between a man standing in a field and a man with a gun standing in a field.

Freeman joined me beside Mom's rock and also contemplated the dead purple locust with a sigh.

"Did you water it?" I asked.

"Yes!" he said. "Twice this week!"

"Uh oh," I replied.

"Wasn't that enough?" he asked.

"It was enough," I said. "Trouble is, I also watered it twice this week."

"I saw Grandpa down here watering too." Freeman added.

We had killed the tree, drowned it, with too much love. We sat there looking at each other, feeling defeated. We could not even grow a memorial tree for our poor, departed mother. What good were we?

A moment later, Ricardo walked up to us, hat in hand.

"Tadeo?" he asked shyly. "Quiero platicar sobre los higos."

He wanted to talk to me about the figs.

I wondered if the figs had a disease, a fungus, perhaps some kind of tree cancer. I worried about those figs like they were the children I had not even sired yet. *If I let Mom's fig orchard die not two months after she left us*, I thought, *she'll kill me!*

"Los higos se miran muy mal. ¡Las hojas se caen!" I replied, telling Ricardo, with panic in my voice, that the trees looked horrible, and the leaves were falling off.

I expected him to reciprocate my concerns, but Ricardo just half-smiled and told me not to worry, adding "¡Ellos van a regressar el proximo año!" meaning the leaves would grow back next year.

I was so embarrassed. *Of course*, I realized. *Figs are deciduous.* They lose their leaves every year at this time and always grow back, just like every other deciduous tree in the world. Embarrassment mixed with relief to create a kind of overwhelming new emotion without a name. I had lived my entire life on this farm and never noticed what the figs looked like in September. I felt like a tourist in my own home. I never had any reason to notice what happened to the figs in the fall before, but now I examined every tree and hedgerow and clod of dirt on this farm with concern and paranoia and a sense of responsibility I had never known.

It was no wonder Mom had always been so busy. Of course, she had not been like other Moms who drove their kids to extracurriculars and attended every single Little League game . . . or even one. With all these plants on the farm to worry about, how could she spare a single moment to think about the people? She did, though. She had always been there for us boys when it really counted. It is a miracle Mom accomplished all she did in her fifty-one short years on this earth.

That moment made me realize I had been so busy stressing about the farm that I had not given much thought to Freeman and his plight, or even to the fact that my classes at Cal Poly would start in a week. I needed to wrap things up here and move back to the house I shared with roommates on Tassajara Street in San Luis Obispo. But what about Freeman? Where was my orphaned teenage brother going to live? Strangely, none of our many relatives were jumping up and down insisting Freeman move in with them.

At that time, Dad was living in his trailer in Davis and would have taken Freeman if asked, but Freeman did not want to go there. We brothers were used to having Dad be peripheral to our lives and knew that was truly the best place for him. Our biological father had become little more than the remembered reason we still had a connection to certain aunts, uncles, and cousins. We knew better than to expect emotional or financial support from him. Sometimes we resented this reality, but we never denied it. We often took advantage of it, though.

Dad's emphasis on doing whatever we wanted made him a prime candidate to supply us with alcohol, marijuana, and, occasionally, magic mushrooms.

Freeman wanted to stay on the farm primarily because it was home, and the farmers' market was a reliable source of income. Isolated as the farm was, living on his own there was a more comfortable choice than some strange trailer park with our all-but-estranged father. There were other details that kept him there too. For instance, if he left, who would take care of his horse, Lucky Ned Pepper?

Shortly after our mother's death, this beloved horse, whom we just called Ned, and who had been a present from Mom, got what looked like a cancerous growth on his ear. We found some cowboy-style vet who literally ripped the growth off with a pair of pliers, but it grew back, so we took Ned to the UC Davis Veterinary Hospital. The vet there told us she could remove the growth again, with the chance that it would grow back again, or else she could just take the whole ear off, to be safe.

Fresh from the loss of our mother to cancer, Freeman and I responded to this news by sharing a glance that amounted to a tacit agreement to cut the ear off. We sure as hell did not want to be defeated by cancer twice in the span of a single year.

Freeman said, "Take the ear!"

As it turned out, the growth was only a sarcoid, a benign tumor, not life-threatening. Later, thinking about how we perhaps overreacted to the problem, Freeman shrugged. It was cancer, after all. We were not going to take any chances. Thinking about all the pain Mom went through, it sure would have been nice if we could have simply "taken the ear off" for her, like we did for Ned.

That very month, the new farm manager Chris and his young family would move into the house where I had been born, where Mom had died, where my placenta was buried under a tree in the front yard, and where Mom's ashes were mixed with the roots of a dead tree in the garden.

Chris's kids would climb the same trees Freeman and I had once climbed and pop wheelies on their bikes in the same gravel driveway. Maybe they would raise chickens in the coop Che had turned into a model airplane shed. Maybe they would plant flowers in the garden where Mom once watered Noah back from dehydration. They would use the same horse trailer on which I had once broken my thumb and drive crops to market in the same stinky, old vans we had filled, year after year, with eggplant, peppers, melons, asparagus, pumpkins, squash, and tomatoes, tomatoes, tomatoes. A new family was coming to run our farm, live on our land, and sort of reenact our life.

I asked Freeman if he was sad about this.

He said, "Hell no!"

I felt exactly the same. All we had ever wanted to do was grow up and leave this farm.

Now, in a way, we were getting the best of both worlds. We got to keep the farm—which we were doing mostly for Mom's memory—and we got to leave the farm too. I had a full ride scholarship to Cal Poly, and Mom's insurance and savings took care of most of Freeman's living expenses and eventual college tuition.

When I asked him about his plans, Freeman told me he had decided to stay on the farm for his senior year but give Chris's family a sense of privacy by staying in a building next door to the house, which we had always called "the barn." It was a two-story building that had a garage, packing shed, and cooler on the bottom floor. Upstairs there was a farm office, bathroom, storage area, and bedroom—all pretty primitive, though.

Aside from our ambivalence about the long-term fate of the farm itself, Freeman and I felt a deep responsibility to our CSA subscribers. They had shown so much faith in us over the years and kept us going both financially and psychologically. In fact, they were the reason Mom, shortly before she died, had happily declared herself "positively middle class," if even for only a season.

Over the course of the past few months, these customers had over-whelmed us with lovingly written condolence cards. Over and over again, their messages recognized Mom as a pioneer in organic farming. They spoke of her bravery in being one of the few female farmers in the region and her determination to build a world where good food, grown well, mattered. These loyal CSA members had subscribed to our local produce delivery, week after week, and we were determined to make sure they got it, at least that year. Next year . . . who knew? We could not think that far ahead.

Having learned quite a bit in the last couple of months about how to set the contents of the home-delivered boxes, I volunteered to take the administrative aspect of this job to school with me. I would soon spend my "study" time selecting the contents of each week's box. I would first look at the list of available farm produce Chris supplied. Then, just as Mom had done, I would complement our selection by sourcing produce from other farms in ever-widening concentric circles, until the box contained a healthy variety of produce. I took great care with this job, as I knew the last thing we needed were our customers looking longingly at grocery store produce departments, wondering why I had only sent them leeks, butternut squash, and turnips.

In the meantime, Noah would continue to handle the bookkeep-ing, Danny would do our produce deliveries, and throughout his last year of high school, Freeman would run the farmers' market stand—something he could do in his sleep by now. As for Che, he did his own thing, flying high above the world, the only one of us perfectly happy to have washed his hands of the farm, lock, stock, and barrel.

"You going to be okay in the barn?" I asked Freeman shortly before leaving for school.

I was not worried about him. It was just that I had been thinking of nobody but myself since Mom's rapid decline began, and I suddenly realized her death had set Freeman up for a potentially hellish last year of high school.

Freeman shrugged. He did not consider his newly meager accommodations that big of a deal.

Grandma and Grandpa On-The-Hill lived right across the street and had said they would keep an eye on Freeman, but they did not offer to take him in. Honestly, we were good students but also wild boys accustomed to an independent lifestyle. I couldn't imagine anyone but Mom being able to manage us as teenagers. So, living in the barn was probably the most practical lifestyle for him. I knew that while Freeman might end up being a bit lonely out there, he had a solid relationship with his girlfriend Carol whose family kept an eye on him too. Freeman also scheduled dinners weekly with the grandparents On-The-Hill. Our brother-like friend Danny, and Chris's family next door, provided additional company.

That year, to stay in touch, we brothers all bought ourselves the latest piece of communications technology: cell phones. Even though we were not getting along that well, the three older brothers were certainly united in our obligation to watch out for Freeman. Over the course of the year, he sometimes needed parental permission for things at school, so he would just sign Dad's name. And if he needed absences cleared up, I would make a phone call to the office myself, posing as his father. In this way, he muddled through. But at one point, Freeman asked me to call the office to clear an absence, and I got more than I bargained for.

"Hi, this is Freeman Barsotti's father," I said. "He missed school today. He had a doctor's appointment."

"Oh! Thank you for calling Mr. Barsotti," said the administrator. "While I have you on the phone, what about last Tuesday?"

"Yeah, that's an excused absence too. Doctor."

"Okay. How about the eleventh, fifteenth, twenty-first, and twenty-fifth of August? And September second, eighth, fifteenth, and seventeenth?"

I was a little taken aback. What could I say?

"Yeah, all excused," I said. "Please clear those up too."

I hung up, and Freeman and I broke down in tears, we were laughing so hard. It was maybe the first time we had taken the idea of operating as bona fide adults to heart. We all knew the drill where education was concerned: get As and Bs, then get into a four-year college. So long as those things were happening, there was not much cause for concern, and his school went along with it.

Looking back, though, I regret not being there more for my younger brother during that painful first year after Mom's death. I found out much later that during the school year, Freeman contracted mononucleosis. His girlfriend Carol's parents took him into their home and cared for him during those weeks. That was nice of them, but it should have been Noah and me. We brothers should have banded together as Mom always insisted. We couldn't, though. Not yet. That year, at the turn of the millennium, all we could do was try to survive the pain of losing Mom, each in our own way.

Truly, it was every man for himself.

On the way south to San Luis Obispo, with all my possessions for the coming school year loaded into the back of the truck, I drove along County Road 19. My arm rested on the sill of the open window as I enjoyed September's warm air breezing through the cab. I passed a sunflower field near the end of its life and noted that its dry, brown stalks, with bowed heads full of seeds, now waited for the harvester. Someone had placed a long row of white boxes that were beehives between the road and the field to pollinate the flowers throughout the summer. They were still there waiting to be moved to their next destination. I could not help but smile, remembering what had once been a field of bright flowers resembling the face of an animal with a thousand yellow-lashed eyes looking straight at the sun.

The golden hills behind the flowers rolled away like an endless sea, and I remembered how Mom once told me scenes like this—not the gold rush of 1849—were the real reason California is called The Golden State. She had been dead fewer than three months, but instead of mourning her in such beautiful weather, I thought enjoying the beauty of a California autumn would be the best way to honor Mom.

The bees were still active, now feasting mostly on the sugar water the beekeeper placed in their hives. As the sun bounced off their translucent wings, I admired their swarms and their diligence. After all, to the bees, this was no peaceful country road. For months, this sunflower field had been their Silicon Valley. As I considered that fact, a splash of moisture hit my face and forearm, followed by a burning pain that shot from my wrist up my arm. Pulling up my sleeve while steering with my knee, I revealed the culprit: a bee's stinger, like a tiny seed, stuck out of the flesh of my wrist. On one end of the stinger balanced a tiny, fleshy bag that was actively pumping poison into me. I flicked the stinger off, wondering about this strange turn of events. After some consideration, I deduced the splash of moisture must have been the stinger's late owner exploding against my truck's side-view mirror and all over my arm, whereupon the bee's back end flew into my shirt sleeve and stung me posthumously. Maybe it was revenge for all the cheap laughs I had earned from folks asking; "What's the last thing that goes through a bug's mind when it gets hit by a car? . . . Its ass!" . . . and apparently, in this case, a vengeful stinger too.

Over the course of that hour, the white bump at the sting site became a red circle that expanded to a four-inch diameter. Then the itching came. Whenever something itches, medical professionals tell you not to scratch it. To hell with that. I enjoyed scratching it. The feeling reminded me how intimately we humans interact with nature and how we are but a small part of a story much bigger than our puny selves.

Chapter Six

·LATE 1980s·

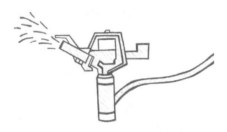

The thirty-foot-long, three-inch-diameter aluminum pipes each had three-quarter-inch-diameter, eighteen-inch-tall risers to which a sprinkler with a hole about an eighth of an inch in diameter sprayed water, imitating rain. The reality of this semi-efficient system was that those eight-inch holes ("orifices" in technical lingo) invariably got clogged. I remember how, as a kid in the single digits, I used to put all these pipes together, then turn on the pump. First thing I did before putting the cap on the end of the pipes was flush the insects, dirt, rodents, and such out of the pipes. To keep myself amused, if there was a farm cat handy, I would grab it and toss it down wherever a scampering rodent was flushed from the pipe, prompting a lopsided gladiator-style fight to the finish. The cat always won.

Then, once all the trash was out of the system, I put the cap on the end of the pipe. When the forty-five to sixty pounds of pressure per square inch pulsed through the sprinklers, the brass nozzles clinked and clanked as they created rain. One clank at a time, the hot dirt became dark with moisture. For a moment, there would be a musty smell that still holds a dear place in my soul. My favorite smell, it permeates the lucky lungs of anyone nearby. Then, just as the amazing smell disappeared, the irrigator faced a second hurdle: many of the sprinklers frequently clogged.

They make filters to prevent such clogging, but our farm, with its unofficial policy of never having the right tool for the job, could not abide such details. So, what I would do as a kid was remove the nozzle from the sprinkler head, suck on it until I got out whatever was blocking it, and spit out the dreck, always peeking to discover what it was this time: dirt? dried vegetation? spider web? If so, with or without the spider? We never panicked—it was always organic! In an effort to stay dry, I would then screw the nozzle back into the pressurized sprinkler, but invariably, I got soaked to the skin. At least that proved it was working! The first objective was to irrigate the crops; the second, to get the job done as quickly as possible. Unfortunately, with each clink and clank, the soil turned to mud, which turned to weights on my shoes, making the walking hard as I tried to get out of the field. Like a lot of farm work, laying those pipes was a very physical experience. I put my whole self into it.

At one point in the late eighties, Dad had saved up a few hundred bucks and decided his boys would not have to spread manure on the fields by hand anymore. He was going to buy us a manure spreader! This was a big deal, and Noah, Che, Freeman, and I piled with Dad into our old, blue Dodge Tradesman van to go pick up this amazing contraption. Ecstatic about the new time-saving purchase, we towed it, clanking all the way home, through a strange, smoky landscape. As often happens in California, a wildfire burned in the distance. The weird orange glow of burning hills on the horizon is something I will always associate with Dad's ill-fated manure spreader.

We got home and attached the manure spreader to our tractor. So far, so good! Next, we tried to figure out how to operate the thing.

There is a giant bin in the machine where you put the manure, so we drove the tractor out to the manure pile and shoveled manure into the spreader, one shovelful at a time, but our production was limited to the child-sized manpower available. That manure bin was huge! It could have held a house full of manure and then some.

We spent hours shoveling manure into the machine's giant maw and did not even come close to filling it. We all watched in excitement as Dad drove off to distribute the manure over the field, but it all fell out in one huge pile. Our dreams of the manure being flung evenly across a wide swath of land were dashed on the spot. In the end, we still had to spread the manure around with a shovel. The damned machine did not save us any time at all! By the time the whole debacle was over, we could have hand-spread all that manure far more efficiently with our old wheelbarrows. Finally, Dad observed that even if he could fix the distribution mechanism, one clearly needs a front-end loader to go along with a manure spreader, and we sure could not afford one of those. So, that manure spreader just sat there by the barn and rusted. We never even used it. Of course, Dad thought the whole adventure was amusing.

Despite these types of frustrations, our father believed that, with the romance of our rural isolation, he gave us an amazing childhood. And he did, in a way. Our life was strange, hard, poverty-stricken, and frustrating, but it was also unusual, all-natural, multicultural, and very, very free. No matter what happened, Dad considered our lifestyle *revolutionary*, more than anything. As hard as life seemed then, I now know that I was born into a kind of club that, provided I showed up and worked hard, would most likely prevent me from ever failing at the game of life in America . . . but I did not know that at the time.

Once, I was at the mall with Dad, getting school clothes, and I picked up a colorful T-shirt that said "*boys!*" across the front in bright neon colors. I thought it was a great shirt for a boy. I was a boy, and it looked cool. I guess I was a pretty literal kid. What did I know?

The teenaged saleslady at the counter was not in the mood for dealing with dumb kids and asked me in a rather condescending tone, "You know this shirt is for girls who *like* boys, right?"

I certainly did not want to wear a shirt meant for girls, and I was just old enough to understand this young woman was on to something, so I put aside the item, but then my father confronted the saleswoman, demanding, "How dare you? My son can buy that shirt if he wants to!"

I wanted to disappear into a hole.

When I think about it now, I am still not sure if Dad was trying to fuel any latent homosexuality I might have had or not. I am, however, grateful to that saleswoman for saving me the humiliation I would have endured if I had showed up to my Esparto public school wearing that shirt. I can just imagine all the devastating nicknames that would have surely followed me through high school.

Dad made it no secret that he would have loved it if at least one of his sons were gay. In the eighties, the gay pride and gay rights movements dominated the news and were always the subject of much public controversy. That was exactly the type of thing Dad loved to be involved with. It would have been a true badge of honor for him to stand up to "the machine" and say, "I have a gay son!"

More than once, Dad told Freeman and me, "You know, if everyone that's gay turned blue, you'd be surprised by how many blue people there are. *You* might even be blue."

Too bad for Dad, we all turned out heterosexual.

On the other hand, my mother once admitted to me, "If one of you boys was gay, it would break my heart."

I was a late bloomer, so, for me, the whole thing was extremely confusing. I had not yet developed my sexuality, and here my parents were at odds about it. I wonder now if they realized then what we know now: that homosexuality and heterosexuality are not choices. All in all, this topic provided for many awkward family conversations throughout the eighties.

One winter, when Mom and I were out walking in the rain, she pointed to a field next to the driveway where the rain ran down a hillside. Each drop of water ate away at the field, leaving the top six inches of soil gone in the same pattern that a river eats away at the earth.

"Sheet erosion!" she declared. "We should take a picture, and you could do a report on it for school!"

I thought, *Why would I do a report on that?* To me, sheet erosion was as common as the fact that the sky was blue. That is just what happens when a lot of water runs over the same piece of bare dirt. I wondered why Mom thought it would impress a teacher to demonstrate knowledge of this obvious fact of nature. But Mom had not grown up on a farm like me. So, she didn't see our home from my perspective. To me, every aspect of the natural world surrounding us was *so obvious*. As a kid, I never realized my mother had grown up in a suburb. She had gone into a lot of debt and taken a lot of risks to move out to the country and give my brothers and me this life. No matter how long we lived there, to Mom, living in Yolo County was fascinating and a great achievement. To me, it was just boring old home.

Throughout my childhood, we simply could not afford more than a few sets of pipes for the whole twenty-acre farm. That is why Noah and Che had to move those pipes, day after day after day, from one side of a field to another, back and forth, back and forth, keeping crops watered. This was such a routine chore for them that their friends stopped coming over to the farm after school because they were always recruited to help. Moving thirty feet of aluminum irrigation pipe after a long school day, in the Capay summer, just plain sucked. Because of this, the twins, Che in particular, reveled in instigating family fights over whose job this really ought to be: theirs or our parents'. Mornings, after school, and weekends, the work never ended, and, for the most part, it never ceased to be Noah and Che's job. Back in the 1980s, when Mom and Dad were helping incubate California's organic revolution, the only help they had was free child labor. Lucky for everyone, they had twins!

The engineer in me wants to make clear that work, technically, is the force required to move a mass over a given distance (work equals force multiplied by distance), while power is the rate at which work is completed (power equals work divided by time). These definitions have helped to give us the term "horsepower," which indicates the power required to move 550 pounds at a rate of one foot every second (one horsepower equals 550 foot-pounds per second). Back when horses were the engines of the day, this was the amount of work a farmer had come to expect from his faithful steed. Horses, unlike people, really do have enough power to move about 550 pounds one foot every second, all day.

In the eighties, however, when Che, Noah, and I were kids, and Freeman just a baby, the farm had no horses. At its best, our seldom-running Oliver tractor was only good for disking and making beds, so the bulk of the farm labor fell to us kids. Mom ran the farm while also taking care of the baby, and Dad put in a lot of time too, but the farm still needed supplemental labor from us three little hippie kids.

In this equation, the child represents a small fraction of one horsepower as he shovels manure into a wheelbarrow, wheels it across a bumpy field, and disperses it onto the soil where it will serve as fertilizer. Considering that the horse of olden times weighed about one thousand pounds and could pull 550 pounds (a bit over half its own weight), then let us assume a seven-year-old weighing fifty pounds is strong enough to move twenty-seven pounds one foot, every second. This will represent "one hippie-kid power," or 5 percent of one horsepower.

The seven-year-old in this equation is me, which means my two twelve-year-old brothers, weighing about one hundred pounds each, could carry around fifty-five pounds per second each, representing "two hippie-kid power" apiece. So, our family had a total of five hippie-kid power or one-quarter of one horsepower to run the farm. By comparison, the average farm in the eighties and nineties utilized the old reliable John Deere 4020 tractor, a ninety-horsepower machine that, with the right attachments, could carry and spread any type of fertilizer across any amount of acreage while its driver drank iced tea and whistled Dixie, barely considering the task "work" at all.

As farmers, we were up against farms whose tractors did the work of roughly three hundred and sixty sets of three hippie kids our ages (1,080 kids total!). Without mechanization, our farm was simply back-breaking labor, and that is the way Noah and Che remember growing up: work, work, work, all the time. Yet, we still managed to grow enough produce to keep a farmers' market stand open all year. For this, we can only thank California's fertile soil, Yolo County's long growing season, and faithful customers who paid premium prices for ugly but beautifully healthy produce.

Growing fruits and vegetables requires a huge amount of physical labor. Even as equipment and technology improve, they have not been able to harvest most of the fresh fruits and vegetables you see in the store. In the produce aisle the only items that are harvested with machines are potatoes, onions, cranberries, baby carrots (actually huge carrots ground up and compressed into little ones) and baby lettuce type items. I am likely missing a couple of items on this list, but my point is that the vast majority of items in the produce isle to this day are harvested by hand, and there is no sign that will change. If those items are organic, that also eliminates the use of herbicides, so we can add in the additional element of hand labor for weed control and thinning of certain crops. Growing organic fresh fruits and vegetables is labor intensive. This is an undisputable fact.

My idealist parents did not know just how much physical labor their farm would require. This was not something taught to them during any part of their education. They did, however, understand that poor people, often from Mexico, were being exploited by agriculture and, correctly, this was one of the items they wanted to see fixed in the food system.

In the late eighties, my parents still hadn't discovered migrant workers, so when the workload grew to more than they and their child labor could handle, they hired UC Davis students to help with the weeding. The first problem with that was the students offered unwanted advice. Running a farm is difficult enough without the weeding crew telling the bosses what to do. The other thing about the student weeding crew was they felt entitled to have lunch provided as part of the job. So, in addition to running the farm and caring for baby Freeman, Mom took care of that too. The final straw came when they routinely complained about the food!

While all this was going on, a Mexican woman wearing a large straw hat came down the driveway one day, asking for work. She showed up every day, on time, and worked hard alongside the college students. When Mom invited her in for lunch with the rest of the crew, she refused, every time, preferring to eat the lunch she had thoughtfully prepared ahead of time. My parents were sold! Happy to do the work in exchange for a fair hourly wage, no "extras" required, Eulalie (we called her Lala) soon became the farm's first, full-time help.

In 1984, my dad saw a couple of young Mexican men driving down Johnny's driveway. He flagged them down, so they came down our driveway instead and asked for work. My parents were overwhelmed, and considering the great impression Lala had already made on them, they hired the boys immediately. That is how they found Ricardo, a Mexican teenager at the time. Soon, Ricardo's cousins showed up, and the farm finally got a reliable solution to its labor shortage.

Not long after they had hired Ricardo and his cousins, my folks met a friendly man named Ramon, who ran the Diamond Lumber Yard in Esparto. Ramon gave my parents deals and advice—a really helpful guy. When Ramon learned about Ricardo and his cousins, he and his wife Lucy turned their barn into a dorm that Ricardo and his cousins lived in while they worked for the summer season. In turn, Dad invited Ramon to sell his walnuts and produce at our stand at the Davis Farmers' Market every Saturday.

Over time, Lala, Ricardo, and Ricardo's cousins changed everything for our whole family. With their help, my folks realized that seasonal field labor paid for itself by getting more done with higher-quality work than either we kids or the UC Davis students could do. This freed my parents up to focus on the business aspect of the farm. Both my parents spoke Spanish, which turned out to be the most practical farming skill they had, as none of that early crew spoke English.

Once the farm had employees, this created a whole new lifestyle for us younger kids. Freeman and I never knew the magnitude of toil Che and Noah had to endure. We certainly had tastes of it here and there, but it didn't define our childhood the way it defined our older brothers' childhoods.

Ricardo introduced my parents to a community of migrant laborers. Like Ricardo, those folks worked every day—harvesting, prepping fields, planting seedlings, you name it—until they got the job done. Our farm desperately needed good help, and these folks were desperate for the work. What's more, working on our farm was a clean, safe environment where they could earn enough money to live and send some home too. When the season was over, these workers were happy to go back to their homes and return to start the cycle again next spring. This seems like a crazy lifestyle to most Americans, but lacking reliable work opportunities at home, what other option did they have?

The heart of a farm is the people who do the hard work in the fields, and I have never known a harder working group of people than farmworkers. During the busy season, they work long hours to keep up with the crops, oftentimes with less than one day off a week for months on end. I remember once noticing Ricardo catching a cat nap in the uncomfortable seat of a tractor. Anyone who could do that must be completely exhausted but also dedicated to his job. With Noah and Che off at college, these few helpers turned into a seasonal crew, allowing Mom to change her management tactics and use me for more delicate tasks.

As Ricardo and the team helped my parents get the work done on the farm in exchange for wages, my parents helped keep Ricardo up to date with relevant policy changes that affected him personally. Back in the eighties, President Reagan created an amnesty program for undocumented immigrants to get citizenship. Mom and Dad knew the rules of the amnesty program well enough to know when Ricardo was eligible for his first driver's license. So, Dad piled Ricardo (in his early twenties, then), my brothers, and me into the blue van and headed for the Department of Motor Vehicles while explaining the good news in Spanish, to Ricardo: "We're taking you to a government office to get a license!"

Unbeknown to us, Ricardo did not comprehend the concept of amnesty at all and had no idea what was going on. As soon as Dad mentioned the DMV, Ricardo literally opened the door and threw himself out of the moving van when it slowed for a stop sign. He thought he was about to get deported! Poor guy.

It all worked out in the end, though. Ricardo got his driver's license and, over the next few decades, with a progressive federal policy and help from our family, Ricardo and his family became United States citizens and purchased their own home in Esparto.

Adults like Ricardo, looking to earn a better living, were not the only people crossing the border in those days. Their kids came along with them. I had no idea at the time, but many kids in my school were undocumented and knew never to discuss their immigration status out of fear of deportation. I did, however, become lifelong friends with one of them. Eric Guerra, an intelligent and charismatic guy, was highly involved, like me, in Future Farmers of America, or FFA. He was on both the FFA Parliamentary Procedure team and the FFA Small Engines team.

Eric's story started somewhere in the eighties when he came from Mexico with his family. In fact, he once shared a memory of that trip with me. He and his brother were in the back of the truck of the coyote who had been paid to smuggle them across the border. But his brother was just a little guy, and when he cried, a woman in the group repeatedly smacked him across the face, telling him to be quiet. Over time, I have heard many stories like this. Such a life isn't easy on kids.

Eric and his family found their way to Esparto, where, while his family worked in the fields, Eric attended school with me. There, he was beloved to everyone. During this time, Eric took jobs after school and one of those was with our neighbor and enemy, Johnny. To this day, Eric still loves to recall how, one day, when he showed up to work, Johnny was not ready for him. In fact, he and a friend were gathered around their illegal moonshine equipment. Johnny's friend looked at Eric, concerned.

"He's good," Johnny assured his friend and immediately put Eric to work picking navel oranges. After a few hours, Johnny approached Eric, saying, "Hey, you hear that?" and pointed past the eucalyptus trees to our house. In the distance, they could hear my mother screaming at us boys at the top of her lungs. They had a good laugh over it!

Today, Eric is known as Councilmember Guerra for the city of Sacramento.

Employing and managing people is at the core of every business, but not all people and jobs are easy to manage. On our farm, this reality was made worse by the fact that Mom would do anything to avoid a confrontation or ugly scene, but now that she had employees, she had to be "the boss." So, one day, she pulled me aside in the kitchen of the farmhouse and put an envelope in my hand. We had a farmers' market employee named Sherry who Mom wanted to get rid of. She did not tell me why, and I didn't ask. At that particular moment, Sherry was unloading the market van.

Mom said, "Thad, please go and tell Sherry this is her last day, and give her this check."

I did exactly as told but was strategic enough to wait for Sherry to finish unloading the van, so I would not have to finish the job myself. I remember the shocked look on Sherry's face. She stammered a reply, but what was she going to do? Argue with a kid? I could tell that if Mom had been standing there, Sherry might have pleaded or made a case for herself and manipulated Mom into keeping her on, but with me, she was stuck. She took the check and left.

By about age seven, I could drive our thirty-five-horsepower Oliver tractor—when it wasn't broken down, that is. We only had two implements for it: a disk and a bed lister. Sometimes, Dad gave me very grown-up chores to do on this tractor, but always with supervision. I do not remember if the Oliver was towing the disk or the bed lister on the day in question, but that year, 1987, Dad used me to make a point to his own father, a PhD and Professor of Entomology at UC Riverside.

That day, Dad's father, Grandpa Barnes, stood out in a field with us after the work was done. Dad said he had to go somewhere, turned to walk away, and shouted back over his shoulder to seven-year-old me, who sat on a running tractor: "Thad, go ahead and detach that implement and put the tractor next to the shed." Then, he walked off without a backward glance, as if tasking a second grader with such a thing was nothing for our family. I was very aware at that moment that Grandpa Barnes was watching me, assessing whether this small human could accomplish such a task.

Feeling self-conscious but pretty sure I could do it, I dismounted the tractor, disconnected two pins that attached the implement, re-mounted, and drove the tractor forward. I was so focused on driving the tractor, which was the part that I thought might go wrong, that I forgot to remove the third pin of the three-point hitch. I carefully pushed the hard clutch in just far enough with my short, weak little legs while using the steering wheel as leverage. I then eased the clutch out and held onto the steering wheel in order to avoid getting flung off as the tractor lunged forward, but as it did so, the implement dragged awkwardly behind and flipped over. Calmly, I stopped and backed the tractor up until the implement was right side up again. Then, I dismounted and removed the third connection pin. Having freed the tractor from the implement, I drove it forward and parked it next to the shed. My little leg was trembling from the effort required by the clutch. Keenly aware that Grandpa Barnes watched my every move, I felt a bit embarrassed by my goof, but still I knew I had pulled it off and was glad. I kept a straight face about the whole thing, just like a grown-up.

I could see in Grandpa Barnes's eyes that he was impressed. Dad's lifestyle on the farm, and the way he raised my brothers and me, mocked everyone in his ultra-white-collar, academic family. So, Dad, the black sheep of his family, often used us boys to make a point about the value of practical skills over intellectual theory. At seven, I did not exactly know what was going on between the two men but correctly perceived this was a test I had better pass.

When I was about eight or nine, Dad took Freeman and me to Point Reyes for camping, and I decided it would be incredibly clever to put a message in a bottle and send it down the stream where we were playing. This is the gist of what I wrote:

This was my best friend Nathaniel's phone number.

My handwriting and spelling were terrible. The neat text above does not accurately represent my almost illegible, terribly sloppy, and badly spelled attempt at a joke. I remember thinking this prank would never get me, or my best friend, in trouble, because I did not write down the area code of his phone number.

I asked Dad for the V8 bottle he was drinking from, washed it out, and shoved the note into it. Freeman and I played with the bottle in the stream for a while, ushering it downstream by poking it with a stick every time it got bound in the branches hanging into the water. Eventually, the bottle drifted away, and we forgot about it.

I didn't think about the bottle again until about six months later, when my mother, holding a cup of tea but wearing a strange look on her face, strolled casually into my bedroom.

"Thad?" she asked, "Did you ever put a note in a bottle?"

Immediately I knew I was going to jail and wanted to burst into tears and apologize, but I kept my cool. Mom laughed, then told me about a phone call she had just received from Nathaniel's father. The whole time, I could tell she was trying to keep a straight face.

Apparently, a foreign child had been kidnapped from somewhere near Point Reyes, right around the time I wrote that note. Somebody found the bottle, read my note, and gave it to the cops. My spelling was so bad that the cops felt sure English was the second language of whoever wrote the note—possibly the very child everyone was looking for! They gave the note to the FBI.

The FBI investigated the phone number. In fact, they tapped the phone lines at my friend Nathaniel's house and put the family under surveillance. Their house was in the country, so it did not take Na-thaniel's dad, Mark, long to notice a guy watching their house with binoculars. He confronted the FBI surveillance crew, and since he had not given the men on a stake-out any reason to be suspicious, they told Mark what was going on and showed him my note. Nathaniel's dad knew my terrible handwriting right away, but he didn't rat me out to the feds. He did tell my mom, though. She thought the whole thing was hilarious, of course—the funniest part being that my terrible handwriting and spelling gave me away.

As a kid, there was nothing I liked better than a ripe, sweet, organic watermelon on a summer day or a white-fleshed peach freshly picked off the tree. However, when it came to cooking the vegetables we so painstakingly sold, I stayed helpless throughout childhood. Mom had dedicated her life to growing healthy vegetables, but the hard work of growing food left her little time to prepare it and none to teach my brothers and me how to do so. Growing up, family dinners had been mostly brown rice casseroles and pork from the pigs we raised for 4-H.

Occasionally, Mom bought us a treat in the form of a box of breakfast cereal and a gallon of milk. We would pound that cereal, with milk and a healthy layer of sugar, for breakfast, lunch, dinner, and snacks. In our house, a box of cereal never lasted more than twenty-four hours. Our love of breakfast cereal was second only to that of frozen burritos. These handheld units of goodness had the benefit of being easy to hide, and we all had our special places in the fridge or freezer to conceal contraband burritos among the healthy hippie food we cared nothing about. There was no better feeling in the world than rummaging through the refrigerator and discovering a brother's secret burrito cache. Finders keepers!

Of course, my brothers and I all knew how to spread butter on whole wheat toast and sprinkle cinnamon and sugar on it. We thought cinnamon toast was delicious, but it made for a limited diet when we were left on our own for hours at a time. We could also make brown rice, though, and cook hamburger in a pan, and we did so over and over. Often such meals were undercooked, burned, or with not enough or too much salt, but we never went hungry.

The summers in Yolo County can be miserably hot. Our house never had an air conditioner, as it was too expensive, so the most relief we got was when we would drag fans into the house and sit in front of them, sweating together like it was a job. We received a little relief from the way the fan evaporated the sweat off our faces, but that was all. It was during one of these Junes that our father decided he would give Mom a break and take all of us kids someplace to escape the heat. The vague plan was to go camping in Northern California.

The five of us piled into our blue van with a bunch of mismatched "camping equipment" and lay down in the back of the seatbelt-less vehicle for the road trip north. Noah and Che were in high school. I was ten. Freeman was six.

In typical Martin Barnes fashion, there was no plan, just the knowledge that an adventure lay ahead. That all changed when Dad saw, silhouetted against the blue sky, 14,180 feet above sea level, the peak of Mt. Shasta. The trip suddenly had a focus. I am sure Dad imagined the accolades he would get when he returned with tales of how he and his four kids summitted Mt. Shasta as a way of getting all-natural air conditioning. After a wet winter, the snow on Shasta was still quite deep.

We stopped at a sporting goods store and rented two pieces of equipment for everyone: boots equipped with crampons (metal spikes that buckle onto boots to prevent sliding on the ice) and ice axes, which came with a brief lesson from the shop assistant on how to hold the axe under your arm as you slid off ice, using the axe to steer your descent or stop you from sliding off a cliff to certain death. The man at the shop shrugged as he rented us the gear, casually assessing whether or not our group was fit for this adventure (we were not), but then deciding he didn't care. It was a sale. Thus ill-prepared to climb a mountain, we then drove to the trailhead. We had no maps (as usual), one canteen, no waterproof clothing, ordinary cotton comforters to serve as sleeping bags, and a blatant lack of relevant experience—all garnished with a sprig of hubris.

Our first goal was to hike to base camp from the trailhead, which turned into quite an ordeal in and of itself. Six-year-old Freeman got tired quickly, so, one item at a time, he shed his load for the rest of us to carry. Despite it being a boiling June in Capay Valley, it was damn cold on the mountain—so cold, in fact, that the thought of overheating in Capay, just a few short hours ago, seemed like a distant memory from a different world. As we slogged through the snow, we all wondered, *if getting to base camp is this hard, how on earth will we make it to the top?*

Before long, we came to terms with the fact that we were lost. In fact, we had never even found the trail in the first place. We had been following random orange spots of paint on the trees, which we thought marked the trail, but in fact someone had marked the trees for logging purposes. The novelty and excitement of walking through the snow evaporated quickly.

Eventually, we stumbled across some footprints in the snow and followed them to base camp, where the camp host expressed abject horror at our intention to summit Mt. Shasta with such meager provisions. We must have been a sight to see with our soaking wet acid-washed jeans, backpacks with the wrong gear haphazardly dangling from it, and no water at all. Dad had never climbed a mountain in his life, and here he was with four kids, no plan, and no gear. Yet, Dad resolved that we would make it to the top.

The camp host had Powerbars for sale. Cash only. Our food situation could be described precisely as such: one box of Bisquick powdered biscuit mix and one box of Oreo cookies, which was to be saved as a reward for when we summited the nearly three-mile-above-sea-level mountain. Dad went to work using his powers of persuasion to convince the camp host to take a personal check and sell him the whole box of Powerbars. Grudgingly, the man agreed and left to get our meager dinner. Personally, I was impressed Dad brought his check book. That was an unusual level of preparedness.

Waiting for the Powerbars, we sat on the cold, wet ground, and night settled in. On the other side of the campground, a huge community fire roared. Around it sat real mountain climbers: fit guys and gals, but mostly guys, with all the proper gear and experience. No kids. We wanted to join them but were too embarrassed to face the pitying glances we would surely receive. So, we rounded up some wood to start a fire of our own.

When the camp host returned with the Powerbars and saw us, his face went slack. Dad had started a fire in a place not designated for fires. Over this illegal fire we were cooking blobs of Bisquick on the ends of sticks, as innocent as could be, while trying to hydrate by melting snow in a lime green plastic canteen over the fire, hoping the snow would melt before the canteen. Then, when the host saw what we were burning, his eyes went wide, he opened his mouth, and no words came out. With a shaking finger, he pointed at the main fuel for our fire: a carefully carved wooden sign that read "Shasta Base Camp."

He stammered, "I . . . I . . . I made that with my own hands!" and showed us the hands in question, as if to help us visualize the hours of labor he had put into the burning sign.

Dad shrugged and took the Powerbars. We gobbled them down like the hungry children we were. Meanwhile, we tried to dry our soaked cotton clothes around the fire, but whatever advantage we gained in drying them we lost by burning holes into them. Any romantic notion we had once entertained about this hike had, by now, completely worn off.

Dad was no quitter, though, so, the next day, we started up the mountain, hiking in our semi-dry denim jeans through the snow with the crampons buckled onto our shoes and ice axes in hand. The hiking was hard. I could barely keep up with my big brothers, and poor Freeman could not keep up at all. Eventually, we realized there was no way we would all make it, so we put together the gear we had and selected Noah to be our representative at the summit. He got our red Jansport day pack, the one canteen, and the coveted box of Oreo cookies. I was very frustrated to see those Oreos go. It had been the carrot that kept me going the whole time. The thought of gorging on a whole box of (otherwise forbidden) Oreos had captured my imagination and focused my effort all day. Nonetheless, Noah forged ahead, Oreos and all, while the rest of us turned around. Heading back to camp was fun, though, because we got to use our ice axes to guide us as we slid down huge stretches of iced-over snow.

When we finally found the blue van again, we waited there for Noah's return. Our first observation was how *easy* the hike to basecamp would have been had we actually been on the trail. In fact, maybe we would all be about to summit Shasta at that moment had we not spent all our energy taking the hard way into the basecamp. By afternoon, though, our focus shifted. Worried about Noah, we asked everyone who arrived off the trail if they had seen our brother. Meanwhile, up on the mountain, Noah was in a bad situation. The precious Oreos were of no use to him because he was so thirsty. Dad had filled the canteen with snow, assuming it would melt over time, but of course it did not melt. There was no reason why, on the freezing mountain, snow would melt just because it was located inside a canteen. Up on the mountain, Noah stopped hiking and pondered his grave situation until a group of college students from UC Davis approached. He told them his problem, and they nicely took him into their group, sharing their water and guiding him to the top, then back down again.

We all escaped Mount Shasta alive, but not without epic sunburns. Hiking in the June sun, at such high elevation, with the white snow reflecting the sun's rays, we turned red as beets. Noah got it the worst. His face blistered and peeled for days afterward, even more than Freeman's and mine. Che, however, had been wearing the beloved Ray Ban aviators he typically wore to project the image of himself as a pilot. They protected his eyes but resulted in him getting a sunburn that left him looking like a raccoon.

Despite my young age, I understood pretty early on in this adventure that we were in over our heads. All the other hikers had specialized gear, backpacks, sunglasses, and multiple canteens, not to mention layers of brightly colored, high-tech-looking clothes and realistic climbing plans. When they saw us kids wearing our everyday jeans and T-shirts, the real mountain climbers on Shasta looked at us in disbelief. But on our farm, it seemed inevitable that no matter what we did, we would be doing it without the right tool for the job. We were used to that state of affairs. However, this trip with Dad was kind of the ultimate (and most life-threatening) manifestation of that. It turned out to be the last adventure we ever had in the blue van. Che made sure of that.

Not long after the trip to Mt. Shasta, Che took the family van joyriding with a bunch of friends. This was the type of troublemaking Noah would normally do, but he was overseas on a school exchange trip working his ass off on a German pig farm. (Turns out, agriculture is a lot of work there too.) Maybe there was a troublemaking vacuum in the air that had to be filled, so Che and his friends went drinking and driving—a typical, potentially deadly, teenage activity in rural America at the time, and maybe still. That van was crap: no back seats, no seatbelts, and it had that nasty compost smell about it, but the kids just needed wheels and were not picky. Spotting them on their way to a party, the local sheriff pulled the boys over. A "good old boy" himself, the sheriff merely chastised them for drinking and driving and told them to proceed directly home.

In the way of teenagers everywhere, my brother and his friends agreed to do so. Then, after the sheriff left, they laughed and proceeded to drive to a party. Later, when they left the party—even more drunk than before—Che reconsidered. His life, as always, was focused on becoming a pilot, and he knew a ticket for drinking and driving could stand in his way, so he took his friend up on an offer to drive the van.

When they approached a certain curve in the road, Che warned his friend, "Hey, there's a forty-five mile-per-hour curve coming up."

The driver, likely the most drunk of the crew, acknowledged that with, "Fuck it! We'll take it at seventy!" and stomped his foot on the accelerator.

The van skidded off the road, rolled several times between telephone poles, slid down an incline, then landed upside down in a waterlogged drainage ditch.

Those drunk kids bounced around in there like socks in a dryer. Some got thrown out the windows, others stayed inside the now-upside-down blue van. Blood splattered everywhere. The driver lay, face down, knocked out, in ten inches of water, in the process of drowning. His ear dangled in the water, not quite cut off from his head. Those who remained conscious stumbled around the field where they had crashed, drunk and shocked, trying to get their bearings.

Someone screamed at the sight of the drowning driver, then grabbed him by the hair and pulled his face up, expecting the worst, but he coughed, clearly still alive. Che snapped back into being the smart, responsible older brother he typically was and looked around for a way to get help. In the distance, he saw one light, so he ran, limping all the way, to what turned out to be a farmhouse. There, he knocked and yelled—desperately, drunkenly, in the middle of the night, scaring the hell out of the house's elderly occupants. They pretended not to be home but called their grown son to come investigate.

Che finally returned to the scene of the accident but left bloody handprints all over the house's front and back doors and first-floor windows. He was lucky not to be shot. When the old couple's son drove to their house, he passed the wrecked van along the way, put two and two together, and called the cops.

In the end, everyone was okay, but they had totaled the vehicle we needed to take our crops to market. Somehow, Mom and Dad bought another van, and the blue van was replaced with a tan van. Mom was justifiably upset about the accident, but she forgave Che. She did, however, make him write and mail a formal apology to those old folks he had frightened half to death. It is hard to say if Che ever forgave himself for the incident, but it certainly left him with a sense of shame. It was one thing to point out to his parents that they should not need his help to do their jobs (as he often did), but it was quite a blow to the entire family's livelihood to total the only vehicle we had to get produce to market. That said, no one died in the accident, and replacing the van was a solvable problem. Life went on.

Che eventually made good on the promise of his aviator sunglasses. Not only did he have his solo pilot's license by age sixteen, before he even had a driver's license, but he was accepted into the United States Coast Guard Academy in New London, Connecticut. The academy provided a path to flying, and he needed that ultimate freedom for himself, having spent his entire youth laser-focused on getting off this farm. The endless toil, the disorganization, the surety of never having the right tool for the job—it was all against Che's very nature. He did not just want to leave the farm, though. He wanted to fly up and away from it, pretty much as close to outer space as he could get.

·FAMILY PHOTOS·

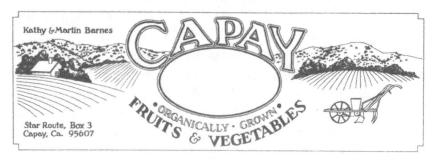

The original produce box labels for the farm. Back when current day CA State Highway 16 was Star Route. These would get stapled onto boxes. Late 1970s.

The blue van! 1974 Dodge Tradesmen with a three-speed transmission. Kathleen, Martin and me or Freeman. Packed up and headed to a Farmers Market to sell Sweet Pea flowers—one of the farm's first cash crops. Mid-1980s.

Me in Grandpa Frank's greenhouse where we grew most of the farm's transplants.
Mid-1980s.

Capay Fruits & Vegetables owns & farms 25 acres that have been organic since 1975. We are located in the beautiful Capay Valley of Yolo County, California. We have been proud members of California Certified Organic Farmers since 1983 and Yocal Produce Cooperative since 1986.

Our goals are to provide the best tasting, healthiest produce we possibly can—and to do it on soil farmed in harmony with the earth, with the help of our valued and respected employees.

Kathy & Martin Barnes & Family
Capay, CA 95607

A postcard made to market our farm's produce at the Davis Food Co-op in 1988.

A view of the farm looking north from the top of the hills. The farm is just west of Capay located in California's rural Western Yolo County.

Me and Mom! Probably about 1983.

My parents during the San Francisco 49ers heyday. Love that Dad is wearing a Joe Montana shirt for the farm photo shoot; #16 is the original GOAT. If you see this Joe, please let me take you to lunch, you are a legend and a big part of our childhood. Notice the original "Capay Fruits & Vegetables" artwork on the old truck.

We are all dressed up for a family photo taken in the backyard of Grandpa Martin's house in Riverside, California where my dad grew up. From left to right: Noah, Kathleen, Freeman, Martin, Thaddeus, and Che. Mid-1980s.

Noah on the left and Che on the right, being kids on the farm. Early 1980s.

Freeman pushing and me pulling a garden cart filled with a sack of seeding potatoes. We are headed out to the fields to plant them by hand. Late 1980s.

Mom sitting in the chair picking a turnip clean to make the perfect bunch. Dad is on the left with his CAFF hat on in his Big Mac overalls, Freeman leaning over his knee. I am on the right. The flowers are status, great for drying.

Top to bottom: Freeman, Thaddeus, and Che.

Left to right: Freeman, Kathleen, Thaddeus, and Che

Country boys selling organic vegetables in the big city! Freeman on the left and longtime family friend Danny Plechaty on the right.

Left to right: Thaddeus, Che, Martin, Freeman, Kathleen, and Noah. Late 1980s.

Freeman and Martin working a beautifully merchandized summer farmers' market.

Selling fall vegetables at the Davis Farmers market. Behind the stand from near to far: Thaddeus, two cousins, Freeman, then Jeff Main (he is in the next stand). Notice the "Yocal" produce box–an early attempt to organize the organic grower in Yolo County that ultimately did not work.

Ricardo Fuentes was hired by my dad in the early 1980s–he still works with us. This photo is from the late 1980s.

The legend, Kathleen Barsotti, in her vegetable patch. Early 1990s.

This was the original cardboard basket that Mom used to make her Farm Fresh
To You boxes—they did not have tops, so getting them all into the van was difficult!
However customers loved opening their doors to find the best local selection
of organic fruits and vegetables leaping out of a basket.

My mom and her parents "Grandma and Grandpa On-The-Hill." From left to right: Lillah Barsotti, Frank Barsotti, and Kathleen Barsotti. Late 1990s.

Terry Schroeder and Kathleen Barsotti. Late 1990s.

A successful fishing trip with Grandpa Martin, Freeman on the left, and me on the
right. This was in the early 1990s, and while Freeman and I were on this trip to visit
our uncle and aunt in Alaska, Mom was having mastectomy surgery
(but we did not find out until we got home).

We had Mom cremated and put her ashes in the front garden of the farmhouse.
After some unsuccessful trees, we planted an acorn that we gathered from
the Mother Oak, a Valley Oak down by Cache Creek.

The first Christmas after mom passed in Puerto Rico where Che, was stationed.
Left to right: Freeman, Thaddeus, Che, and Noah.

Puerto Rico party–this was the preamble to the big brawl.
Left to right: Thaddeus, Che, and Noah.

Heirloom Tomatoes at a farmers' market. We started calling the farm
"Capay Organic" after mom passed; her name for the farm was
"Capay Fruits & Vegetables", which we called "CFV."

The new Farm Fresh To You logo with the Golden Gate in the background.

After Mom passed we created a real logo for Farm Fresh To You—here are those boxes in the original packing shed.

This is one of my favorite photos of the four of us, from left to right: Freeman, Noah, Thaddeus, and Che. We are moving into an apartment we rented at 2233 Leavenworth Street in San Francisco. The Bubble Van, tattooed up with the Farm Fresh To You logo, was the moving vehicle. Early 2000s.

Me looking tired in a tomato field. Early 2000s.

Me on the left and Freeman on the right, looking country AF. Early 2000s.

Family photo at the farm in 2022 with the third generation.
Left to right: Imogen, Ainsley, Freeman, Jamison, Carol, Everly, Che, Camille, Sammy, Noah, Aurora, Jonah, Kate, Lucca, Thaddeus, Julien, Moyra, and Lola.

Family photo taken 2022.
Left to right: Lola Che, Thaddeus, Julien Francis, Moyra and Lucca McRae.

Chapter Seven

·OCTOBER 2000·

Throughout October of 2000, college seemed so irrelevant to my life that my attendance, studies, and test scores suffered. With my mental and emotional energy focused on the farm and Farm Fresh To You, I also dealt with what was, to me, an incredibly difficult course load that quarter, including calculus, dynamics, physics, and chemistry. My department, Bioresource and Agricultural Engineering, had its own study room for the department's students. In that room, a good group of peers provided a sense of belonging and the opportunity to develop relationships with the other students in my department. On top of that, both this year and the previous one, I had found—to my surprise, really—that socializing "out in the world" was not easy. This place was a big change from life on the farm. In San Luis Obispo, I stumbled through this new phase of my life and felt perpetually in transition.

I had lived my whole life in rural Yolo County, socializing only with my family, a few select friends, and the farm team. My brothers and I did not fit in among the Waldorf-school kids at the farmers' market groups, nor did we feel much of a sense of belonging with the kids our age at school. We didn't intentionally keep to ourselves, but our family and way of life were so different that it made it hard to relate to others. In college, though, I had to find a way to make friends (and girlfriends), tongue-tied as I was, or be all alone. As a result, I had my fair share of being alone. I didn't mind it much but also recognized it was not healthy. Alcohol would prove to be an amazing lubricant to solve this whole situation.

Back in the department study room, I used to do my homework along with the other students, but they had no idea that before I started the homework, I first had to figure out the weekly contents for the Farm Fresh To You boxes. This required understanding what produce was available from our farm, determining what other produce would supplement our farm's selection, placing the orders for produce that was not coming from our farm, then writing a Farm News article for our newsletter.

My newfound knowledge of Excel was very helpful in creating the weekly box contents, and, to this day, the original spreadsheet I created for Farm Fresh To You, with significant revisions, is still used to set the best selection of produce for each week.

Though it had only been a couple of months since I left the farm for college, I developed a habit of driving back to the farm as often as I could. At one point in October, I played hooky from Cal Poly and drove up to the farm to "supervise" the seeding of the cover crops. Cover crop seeding is not difficult, and my supervision was not needed, but the issue of cover cropping had become rather close to my heart lately. Mom and Dad used to have an ongoing argument each spring, where they tried and failed to determine whether it was necessary to chop the cover crops and disk them back into the soil while they were still green (Dad's opinion) or if one could just let them dry in the field, then disk them back into the dirt any old time (Mom's opinion). To me, growing up, the cycle of planting cover crops in the fall, chopping them dead with a farm implement in the spring, listening to my parents argue about them, and eventually disking them back into the soil, was as predictable as the sun rising and setting. Watching Ricardo drive a tractor across the neatly disked field, drilling the mix of legumes (cow peas, vetch, and fava beans) that was our cover crop mix into the soil, I pondered my education and the concept of cover crops.

There is a hearty and ongoing debate within the California agriculture community over which university is the best. UC Davis has a research culture focused on finding the limits of theoretical possibilities for agriculture. Their professors claim *their* research will unlock the solution to feeding the world, and they do so with a perception of being above Cal Poly, a state school that focuses on real-world agriculture in terms of actually farming and feeding people *today*. Cal Poly's approach has no focus on research and takes a learn-by-doing attitude, paying close attention to emerging new technologies and how those are working on real farms. At the end of the day, though, this school's goal is to build real things and get yields from resources—real yields, the kind that feed people and put money in the bank, not the theoretical kind. Having always had boots on the ground, I saw the value of an undergraduate degree that taught these real, tangible skills. Now, I wholeheartedly agree that Cal Poly (my school) is a better undergraduate agriculture school. That said, my parents and brother were UC Davis folks, and it was through this contrast in philosophies that, in the year 2000, I found myself pondering the place of cover crops in agriculture.

My education thus far had recently provided scientific evidence as to the value of cover cropping, the kind of evidence that had made its way into Cal Poly's empirical, tried-and-true knowledge of farming. Legumes, when grown and tilled back into the soil, add organic matter and nitrogen to the soil, which develops more healthy soil, which aids in improved crop growth and reduces the need to buy fertilizer. I was slightly dumbfounded to realize that my parents were right on this. When they had been at UC Davis, all this stuff was still theoretical, so, I wondered, what other hocus-pocus practices were they right about?

At Cal Poly, in my parents' day, all information about organic farming was still considered "crazy hippie stuff," and it was laughed at.

Growing cover crops, using pheromones to disrupt the mating cycles of pests, burying cow horns in the soil when the moon is just so, rotating crops, making compost—it was all lumped together and laughed at.

A lot of those methods are now established organic farming practices, but not all. For instance, I find the "biodynamic" practice of burying cow horns pretty superstitious and, frankly, mildly entertaining. When I think about farmers supposedly living so in tune with their fields that they could time their cow-horn burials in sync with the moon, seasons, and plantings, I simply want to ask: is it the cow horns or these farmers' attentiveness to their environment that make their crops grow so well? I would bet on the latter.

Cow horns and genuine hocus-pocus aside, the tide was beginning to change when I returned to my classes at Cal Poly in the year 2000. My professor Dr. Burt drove home this reality with his lectures on the benefits of growing cover crops, which provide up to five hundred pounds per acre of nitrogen. The other reality Cal Poly taught was that organic crops fetch more money. As a result, these huge farming outfits (whose kids all went to Cal Poly) wanted a piece of it. Slowly, more and more of the growers started what they called "growing a line of organics." A change in the industry was happening.

Thinking back to my parents' annual argument, I asked my teacher if cover crops had to be tilled back into the soil while still green or if they could dry out first. He replied that legumes used for cover cropping team up with rhizobium bacteria to take nitrogen from the air and turn it into solid nitrogen on little nodes on their roots. After the plants are chopped and disked into the earth, the nitrogen will not be released immediately. Instead, it breaks down slowly over time to provide nitrogen for future crops. Therefore, the method by which the crop should be incorporated back into the soil was a moot point. Either way would work.

I loved the irony of the fact that my parents were doing something right but disagreeing over the process when both methods had the same effect. Nevertheless, I could just about hear Mom chuckling with pride and rolling her eyes when I discovered this definitive proof that her farming practices were cutting edge. The experience made me realize my parents were not the bumbling farmers they had always seemed to be. They might have lacked knowledge of certain details and skills, but they were leaders in the fundamentals of organic farming.

Mom and Dad had both attended graduate school at UC Davis in the seventies, when synthetic fertilizers, pesticides, and herbicides were all the rage. Knowledge of farming without the latest and greatest chemical tools had been hard to come by in that environment, so even though UC Davis was a heavyweight agriculture school back then, my parents' educations did not do them a whole lot of good. In their day, organic growers were all going by the seat of their pants. Not so, nowadays. Thanks to people like my parents popularizing organic farming, knowledge of things like cover cropping is pretty much in the mainstream now. With today's mature organic farming industry, organic materials including fertilizers, pesticides, and services are mainstream too. As a student at Cal Poly, I easily found information, products, and services that had eluded my parents for years.

As I built the spreadsheets that helped me organize Farm Fresh To You, I consulted Mom's old notebooks as well as my own instinctive knowledge of the produce and its various harvest dates. Mom had been right there on the farm, elbows deep in the packing of each box, so using handwritten lists was good enough for her, but with me at Cal Poly (designing the selection for each box), Noah living in San Francisco (handling bookkeeping), Freeman finishing high school (while running our farmers' market stand), Che flying high above it all, and our farm manager Chris still getting his bearings, we could not keep the farm running Mom's way anymore. Although this was just four months after her death, harvests do not take grief sabbaticals, so we had to each do our part. That meant trusting each other and learning where the lines in the sand were, one disagreement at a time.

Around this time, Mom came to me in another dream. We walked side by side in a long, narrow room. She was healthy in the dream, like her old self, but as we walked closer to the other end of the room, tears came to my eyes—at first a little, then more and more until I sobbed uncontrollably. At the end of the room lay Mom's sick and dying self in a hospital bed. Healthy Mom had taken me to see sick Mom, as if it were her duty to guide me to the Valley of Death.

Compared to other country boys, I was a late bloomer in the realm of drinking and smoking weed—two staples of life for rural California kids. It was not until I left Capay and lived away from home that I realized the country folks of the Capay Valley were onto something with their boozing. Turns out, I really liked getting a little out of control, occasionally. This proved to be a good excuse to let those maudlin emotions out and was also a way to bond with my older brothers. It narrowed, if not eliminated, our age differences.

Back when Che and Noah were teenagers, just learning about beer and women and such, our seven-year gap in age left their world a mystery to me, but when I finally got old enough to seek those things out, my big brothers were there for me, inviting me along with open arms.

In fact, I remember the exact moment when my older brothers realized I was ready to be included in their young-adult world. They were home for the holidays, and we were returning from Woodland. Che was driving, Noah was in the passenger seat, and Freeman and I were in the back. When we pulled up to the stop sign inside Madison, I asked them out of nowhere, "Hey guys, what's a clitoris?"

A deafening silence filled the white Plymouth Colt as the realization that little Thad was growing up hit my brothers like a ton of bricks. Then they both exploded with whoops of laughter and encouragement. With what I am sure now was limited knowledge of the subject, they candidly discussed what they knew about the topic. Che explained his realization that growing up where we did, with all brothers, Mom was the only girl we knew, but none of the girls "out there" are "like Mom." I think this was his way of trying to tell me that none of us had any clue about women. Noah agreed that growing up on the farm had done nothing to prepare us for understanding or relating to women. I left that car trip more confused than before, but the conversation opened the first chapter of my grown-up relationship with my older brothers.

Unbeknown to me at the time, Freeman listened to that conversation with ears wide open. He paid attention to everything his brothers said and watched everything we did. So, when he finally got to be a teenager, Freeman had gained a certain amount of savvy that made him quite a bit more sophisticated than the rest of us had ever been.

Before Mom died, when I was a college freshman, I used to visit Noah and Che whenever I drove through San Francisco. They would sneak me into bars, and we would all fail miserably at attempts to meet women. The three years of age that separated Freeman and me was far less than the seven-year trench between me and my older brothers, so Freeman often joined us, too, and participated in the debauchery. We had some good times, just us boys. That was our way—we fought a lot but forgave a lot, and the forgiving came easier when beer was involved.

Come the fall of 2000, my drinking was no longer just a partying thing or a pleasant social lubricant. It became, for the first time, a big part of my life. If I was not working or studying, odds were good I was drinking. At this point, whenever we boys got together, there were always beers. As often as not, a few turned into as many as possible. I have memories of being too drunk to responsibly drive but doing it anyway. Looking back, I would even say I drove with a subtle degree of suicidal intentions, flirting with the idea that an easy way out of all my life's stress could be a telephone pole.

It was hard to not think endlessly about Mom: things I regretted not saying to her, conversations I wished we had had, and so many missed opportunities. I felt sorry for myself. For some reason, it did not cross my mind that my careless behavior endangered others. It never occurred to me how selfish I was being. Looking back, what I did shocks me. I can't imagine acting like that now, but back then, I drank without thinking. I drove without thinking. The combination of thinking and feeling that used to be just a part of living now seemed excruciating, unbearable. I had to blot out both my heart and brain. Alcohol did that for me.

I would wake up the morning after a binge and contemplate the fact that I had done some dangerous—maybe even suicidal-ish—stuff, but I didn't stop. I didn't care. Mostly, I just didn't realize any of it mattered. After all, Mom was not there to worry about me. Dad had moved on, long ago. As for my brothers, we were all in our own little bubbles of grief, isolated from each other but trying to keep in touch, kind of. So, who really cared what the hell I did? I just kept living that way with no end in sight. Looking back at that lifestyle now, it makes my stomach turn to realize how out of touch I was with my emotions.

I had originally selected Cal Poly because Mom told me I would like it there. I trusted her, so I applied there and to Texas A&M as a backup school. When I got accepted to Cal Poly, I enrolled without even visiting, based solely upon trusting Mom's opinion. She said it would be a good school, and that was all I needed to know. Cal Poly makes you select a major when you apply, so I took Mom's advice on how to do that too.

She told me the way she had selected a major was to look at the course catalog, read the descriptions of the classes required for each major, and select the major that had the most interesting-sounding classes. Based upon that advice, I selected BRAE (BioResource and Agriculture Engineering), which is an accredited engineering major with a focus on agriculture. What I would eventually do with a BRAE degree remained a mystery.

My primary contact with Grandma and Grandpa On-The-Hill in October of 2000 was the occasional weekend visit, where they would often take me to a church function. This was traditional, as, back when we were kids, our grandparents took the family to Catholic church every Sunday. So, one weekend that fall of 2000, I attended a dinner in the church hall with my grandparents and Aunt Dianna. As we sat and listened to my cantankerous Grandma expound upon *exactly what is wrong with the world*, an older lady I did not know approached our table. She introduced herself as Ellen and asked if she could sit in the vacant seat.

Ellen had peculiar, drawn-on eyebrows. Irregular red spots mottled her pale skin. Her crooked teeth looked too big for her face, and I suspected her flowered pink hat concealed a balding head. I recognized a chemotherapy patient immediately. Although she was physically frail, Ellen's strong, blue eyes projected the intensity of the life she still had in her.

When she asked to sit at our family table, my grandparents, Aunt Dianna, and I shared an uncomfortable look. We did not want Ellen, with her hovering Angel of Death, anywhere near us, but each of us quickly assured her she was welcome. In fact, we went overboard to treat her like a long-lost friend, trying to compensate for our initial hesitation.

When Ellen talked to us about her grandchildren, those blue eyes really lit up, and I felt glad that she got to live this long and enjoy something that brought her as much happiness as those kids did. The conversation even gave me hope. Perhaps, I thought, grandchildren really were that great, and living until I saw my own would give my life purpose too.

Back at the farm, after dinner, Freeman and I hung out in the barn where he was living. With Chris and his family occupying the farmhouse, Freeman fended for himself pretty well out there. His room had a hodge-podge collection of the things someone needs to live in one room. There were two single beds, dirty clothes everywhere, a portable heater, family pictures hanging here and there, a microwave with dirty dishes stacked on top, a mini fridge, and, to round out the picture of the teenage bachelor life, an overflowing trash can.

Despite the look of the place, Freeman told me things were going fine. He ate dinner with the grandparents every Thursday. At school, he was student body president and a member of the wrestling team. He also had his close friend Danny to rely on as well as his girlfriend Carol, who would become his wife many years later. So, despite living on the farm alone, without parents or siblings in his day-to-day life, Freeman was active, busy, and doing just fine.

If I were in Freeman's shoes—isolated on the farm at sixteen—I probably would have hauled in a pile of junk food and indulged myself like a maniac. Instead, my brother had learned to bake lasagna for his weekly dinners with the grandparents. In fact, I had a feeling that Grandma and Grandpa On-The-Hill were not watching over Freeman so much as he was watching over them. Our grandparents were stoic types who met during World War II and never spoke to us of the hardships they endured growing up, or any aspect of their private pain. We knew, though, that they grieved deeply for their eldest daughter. Grandpa, especially, had to stuff his feelings away, because now he had to care for his declining wife.

Freeman had not wanted to attend the church dinner that night. He was not a big fan of church. I wasn't either anymore. Going to St. Martin's was now just a habit and a way to bond with my grandparents, but things had not always been that way. As kids, we didn't know any life but that of being devout Catholics. I never questioned the authority of a priest or nun and took what I learned in Catechism as fact.

Mom had designed the barn, with its red metal roof, to replicate the type of old barns found in the area. It was tall and square, and when the October winds blew, they really rattled the walls. That evening after the church dinner, Freeman and I sat in his room in silence for a while, just listening to the angry weather outside. Clouds had rolled over the land all day, and now, with nightfall, rain fell hard and fast, pummeling the windows. This hard rain would persist throughout October and November and fill up the aquifer with the water we would use all year long, but once the winter rains started, the farm practically ground to a stop. Tractors cannot function in mud. I remember how, on rainy days, Mom suffered the frustration of not being able to get any work done.

Even more so than rain, wind in the Capay Valley has always foreshadowed the season change. Whenever the wind howls, stress settles into my soul as I think through all the things the wind may be ruining at that very moment. It reminds me how out of control I am and how insignificant we all are when confronted with nature's awesome power. As Freeman and I listened to the wind howl, the scent of fall rain filled the air and gratified our souls with an intense sense of place and season. We smiled at each other. This scent meant home. It was, in fact, our true church.

The scent of Yolo County rain meant being protected by Mom and being together. It meant that no matter how the summer harvest had gone, we were in a new season now, giving us a new start and fresh opportunities to succeed. It meant time to rest. No matter how frustrating it was to pause in fulfilling the farm's endless demands, nature forced us to take a break, to huddle together in the safety of home, and to appreciate each other. I fell asleep, mid-conversation, on the floor of the barn.

The next morning, I remembered how the sight of the farm on a morning after rain was even better than the scent of rain itself. When Freeman and I wandered outside to breathe it all in, we noticed that, typical of October, the rain had left no puddles. The thirsty ground soaked up everything. We would not experience standing water or run-off until December, when the ground would finally be saturated.

Beneath a sunny sky now filled with white cloud bunnies, Freeman and I checked the Napa cabbage. It had survived the storm nicely. In the next field over, fennel fronds waved in a light breeze, looking like the surface of a roiling ocean. Freeman observed that the fennel bulbs were still a couple of weeks from harvest, and I agreed. Finally, we moved on to a favorite oak tree, surrounded—as usual this time of year—with an extensive pumpkin patch.

The magnificent oak's stout branches arced over the pumpkins like a mother hen protecting her chicks. It saddened me that I would not be there to see the excited children of our CSA members running around the field, picking out the best pumpkins for their jack-o'-lanterns during the scheduled fall visit, but I had to get back to school. By now, the skin on my hands had finally grown back normally, and I reminded myself that along with the fun times on the farm came a level of responsibility that had nearly undone me back in the summer. Even though San Luis Obispo would not ever have the same musty smell of dry Capay soil getting its first rain, I felt relieved to be able to throw my knapsack in the car and drive away from the farm, with its greenhouses to manage and fruit trees to prune. Leaving made me feel pleasantly but unnaturally free.

I remembered the water management issues that come with this time of year. The pump had to be placed in the creek so that we could continue to water baby greens even though the canal would soon stop running. Also, there were six-foot-high tomato stakes to take down. Delaying on even one of these crucial tasks could have a snowball effect down the line. If you do not get those stakes out of the ground, the earth will not be ready for cover cropping over the winter months, which has to be done within a specific window of time. Farming is about timely execution, which only comes when you plan and prepare.

Chris, who was an experienced farm manager who I trusted completely, would handle all of it, but I still could not stop stressing, thinking about everything that needed to be done. I wanted to leave this farm behind me. I really did. I wanted to be my own man with my own career and life, but letting go of the farm was like cutting an umbilical cord that had refastened itself after Mom's death.

Mom's dead tree still stood, a bit crookedly now, in her garden out front. It made me sad, and I vowed to replace the tree next time I came home. For now, though, I needed to get out of that place or my hands were going to start peeling all over again.

A couple of weeks later, I knew from experience that the kale and chard—which had only been six inches high when I last visited the farm—would be a foot and a half tall now and ready to harvest. As I sat in the study room at the Cal Poly library, calling other farmers to supplement what I knew was coming off our farm, I got a little excited thinking about our customers opening their boxes to find the big, fluffy green leaves they loved so much, but I did not have the luxury to daydream. Once I finished the CSA spreadsheet, engineering homework called.

My grade point average slipped considerably that year. I could hear Mom telling me, "In our family, we get As and Bs," but now Cs sounded amazing, and D even had a nice ring to it. It just meant I was *done*. My brain felt full, both academically and emotionally. My head was like a cornucopia spilling over with vegetables, mathematics, loneliness, physics concepts, harvest schedules . . . all mixed together in a confusing tangle.

Chapter Eight

·EARLY 1990s·

After more than a decade of living out in the Capay Valley, Mom had become a true steward of the earth. She loved being a farmer and a parent and aspired to be successful at this work, which meant coupling both agrarian and financial sustainability to provide for her family. As she moved forward with this ambitious new understanding of life, Dad was still the man she had fallen in love with and married so long ago. He was perfectly content with the fact that he had never developed past being an angry young man constantly fighting "the machine." Mom, however, had moved on from fighting society's ills to building the new world she had always envisioned. Settling down and focusing all his efforts on the farm and family would have been contrary to Dad's essential nature—after all, there were always new crusades that needed his attention, and he loved living on the edge, financially. By the early nineties, it was clear that each of them envisioned a different future for their relationship and family. In their efforts to make these very different needs known to each other, they fought often.

When I was ten, in 1990, Mom got diagnosed with cancer and had a mastectomy. That is when she realized the stress of trying to hold our family together was killing her. By the next year, my parents had worked out an amicable-ish divorce. Mom borrowed money from her parents to buy Dad out of the farm, and they worked out an arrangement where Dad would continue to do the farmers' market, which he was so good at. With this arrangement, Freeman and I would have a chance to see him on a regular basis. Noah and Che, who had recently moved out to begin college, learned about the new arrangement through phone calls and letters.

Before the divorce, Dad had already taken up with a British girlfriend named Renée who he met while she was interning at a neighboring farm. Renée had a knack for retail, and they worked the farmers' market together. I have memories of being with Dad at the farmers' markets while he wooed or attempted to woo other, often younger, women he met there. Mom soon found Terry, another local organic farmer, so, relatively quickly, my parents officially separated and aligned themselves with other partners. Terry never moved in with us, but Mom used to sit and talk to him on the phone in the evenings. They talked a lot about vegetables, fruits, and farming, and by the tenor of Mom's voice, I could tell she was happy.

At first, Freeman and I were horrified by all this sudden change, but when we woke up and went to bed each day without hearing a single argument in the house, we realized the change was definitely for the best. Having Dad on the periphery of our lives instead of at the center was also better. We loved him, but even at a young age, I understood there was something about Dad that made him a little childish. While we were not asked to pick sides, I could sense the tension between my parents and always knew I was on my mother's side, one hundred percent.

Not long after the divorce, Dad—spontaneously, while visiting Europe with Renée—bought a ruin in the South of France that he planned to restore. After all, the money he had received from selling Mom half the farm was burning a hole in his pocket. He also had a mobile home in Davis, California, where he could stay when he came stateside to see his sons, participate in the farmers' market, and operate his countercultural newspaper, *The Flatlander*. So, he had a finger in every pie, a wife twenty years his junior, a project to work on that kept him away from the family, and a venue in print form that fulfilled his need to tell everyone else why they were wrong about everything . . . in short, everything he loved.

With Dad spending so much time in Europe, we saw him less and less. My brothers and I never talked too much about the new situation, but I think it is fair to say that none of us exactly missed Dad. He was a part of us, and we had a lot of fun memories together, but with life out on the farm being so hard, Dad had mostly just made it harder. Che and Noah left the farm right before the divorce: Noah to UC Davis and Che to the US Coast Guard Academy. So, their lives did not change much because of our parents' split. As for Freeman and me, we grew to like having Mom all to ourselves. Of course, we had no idea that settling into a one-parent lifestyle meant that, for all intents and purposes, we would be without any parents at all a decade later.

After the divorce, Mom legally changed her name from Barnes back to Barsotti, and I changed mine, too, in solidarity, even though I was only fifteen. Freeman soon followed suit. Our older brothers had already started their adult lives with the Barnes name, though, so they kept it. Dad was cooperative about this. He signed the necessary court documents and did not ask any questions. The names alone tell the story of our family's chaotic beginnings: two brothers named Barnes, two named Barsotti, yet all with the same parents.

Naturally, Kathy and Martin's divorce and their subsequent recoupling with other farmers hit the farmers' market gossip grapevine. The community supported all of us, but somehow that place had always been more Dad's "scene" than Mom's. While Dad was energized by the fun of the market, for Mom, going to market had always been a stressful, all-day event, at the end of which she would be exhausted. Even with Dad and Renée doing a great job at the markets, Mom was able to do a cost-benefit analysis of the time and expense of hauling our wares to market once or twice a week and realize the farm would benefit a lot from finding a better way to sell produce.

She put a lot of energy into seeking alternative venues for produce sales, and eventually, we built up a relationship with some produce wholesalers in San Francisco who started regularly buying our fruits and vegetables. Making deliveries to their warehouses was a two-hour drive each way, but there, we sold the same amount of stuff as at the farmers' market, only instantly, instead of over the course of many hours. These wholesale sales were definitely a step up, but still not enough for the sea change Mom needed to make the farm truly sustainable. Finally, Mom had a revelatory conversation with a friend named Bill Brammer, the owner of the organic farm Be Wise Ranch in Southern California. An idea that had been working for him—community supported agriculture (CSA)—planted a seed in her mind that quickly grew.

Mom started our CSA program, Farm Fresh To You, in 1992. The box was technically named Capay Fruits & Vegetables with the tag line "Farm Fresh To You," but the tag line quickly morphed into the name of the business, which was always written as FFTY. Noah and Che, having left home already, never got to experience the lifestyle changes that came with the program's success, but I remember this transition well. It all began when a woman named Sibella Kraus wrote an article in the food section of the *San Francisco Chronicle* explaining the concept of community supported agriculture and Capay Fruits & Vegetables' new initiative from Yolo County. Her article made a point of the fact that our program included home deliveries for subscribers. It also included the only phone number we had ever had: our home landline.

The morning that article hit the newsstands, our phone rang off the hook. Mom got so overwhelmed with answering it that she had nine-year-old Freeman stay home from school and man the phone all day. I couldn't believe it! All these strangers wanted to give us money, and for what? Vegetables?

Freeman and I were living on a diet of brown rice casserole, cinnamon toast, and vegetables, garnished with fresh fruit in the summers. Having grown up with such an oversupply of vegetables, we were never motivated by them. In fact, I had spent countless hours musing over their relative worthlessness. At one point, as a child, while riding my bicycle past our fields, I remember daydreaming about a scenario where everyone in society would produce something they were good at producing and everyone got to have whatever they wanted. It seemed like a reasonable economy to me. If this were true, we could give vegetables to whoever wanted them, and in return I would get a four-wheeler. It would be a decade later when I learned that Marx, following the communist revolution, argued a similar idea. With the proletariat in control of production, after a period of transition, a classless society and economy of common ownership would emerge and form equilibrium. It would be "from each according to his ability [my endless supply of vegetables], to each according to his need [I definitely *needed* a four-wheeler]." Philosophical discussions regarding the best way to organize an economy aside, we kids did not get what the excitement was about but understood that vegetables were finally bringing some value to our family.

That day, Mom found her people: conscientious consumers a lot like herself, people who cared about where their food came from and wanted a relationship with the natural resources and people who grew it. In many cases, these consumers, residing in in the Bay Area, overlapped with our farmers' market customers. The one thing they all had in common was that they wanted a better selection of local produce, they wanted it to be free of chemicals, and they could afford to pay a bit extra for the peace of mind that comes with fueling their children's bodies with great-tasting, vitamin-rich, chemical-free organic food. On the phone that day, Mom at first, then Freeman, promised each subscriber that our produce was the best around. The callers would not be disappointed.

Some callers, though, were skeptical. They doubted we could provide weekly boxes of local food all year long, so Mom explained her concept. These callers thought eating local meant that in the low season, their boxes would contain nothing but turnips, leeks, beets, and last season's stored squash and potatoes, but Mom explained that she had a much more practical concept of "local" than that.

"You will always get a great selection of greens, fruits, and roots, no matter what time of year it is," she said, adding, "First, we look at what our farm has to offer. Then, if needed, we supplement that with produce from other farms, looking outward in concentric circles as far as we need to make an excellent selection, but as soon as something more local becomes available, that gets priority. We promise that you will never look longingly at the produce aisle of your local grocery store."

She urged the callers to imagine a map of the Western US, then draw a circle encompassing fifty miles outside the Capay Valley. When needed, we would purchase vegetables from other farms within that circle to enhance the Farm Fresh To You boxes. If nothing interesting could be found within a fifty-mile radius, we would reach out further to farms within one hundred miles, and so on, always keeping the supply domestic.

When Capay Valley summers were too hot for greens, we got them from the cool summer fields in Salinas. When the last of our citrus was done for the winter, we would supplement the box with delicious apples and pears from the Pacific Northwest. When it was too wet and cold in Salinas for vegetables, they came from California's desert. When the season dictated, subscribers would taste Ataulfo mangos from Southern California, cranberries from the bogs of Oregon, or vine-ripened heirloom tomatoes from Capay. This was all packed into the Farm Fresh To You boxes along with a newsletter talking about what was going on with our farm and a few recipe ideas for the produce in the box.

"Eating local," Mom assured her callers, "does not mean being stuck with what can only be grown in your own backyard."

Our concept of "local" would expand and contract, as needed, with the seasons. People liked the simple practicality of that idea and signed up for Farm Fresh To You in droves.

At one point, during that initial onslaught of phone calls, our overwhelmed mother had to tell Freeman to put subsequent callers on a wait list. In less than a day, she had literally signed up more subscribers than she could feed.

"What? A wait list?" protested a flabbergasted Freeman, who could not conceive of turning down money for any reason. His shoes were duct-taped together just like mine, and even at nine years old, like the twins and me, he constantly schemed for ways to make a buck. In no time flat, Farm Fresh To You became our farm's primary source of reliable revenue and the CSAs subscribers a whole new community for the farm.

The same summer Mom started the CSA, when I was twelve, I flew with Dad to Europe for a month. We landed in Heathrow, stayed for a couple of weeks at my stepmother Renée's flat in London, then crossed the channel on a ferry, took a train part of the way to Dad's place in the South of France, and biked the rest of the journey. At the end of the trip, we planned for Dad to remain in Europe while I traveled back to the US alone. Dad was supposed to get me back to the airport in London, but at the last minute, he did not see the point of crossing the English Channel just to cross back the other way on the same day, so Dad put me on the ferry by myself.

My instructions were to catch a train to London when I got off the ferry. From there, I was to take the tube to a town where Renée had an empty apartment. I had a key to the apartment and could walk there from the train station. I would stay the night there by myself and finish the train ride to Heathrow the next day, where I would catch my flight home. The whole arrangement was a combination between Dad not wanting to be bothered with the hassle of taking me to the airport and him trusting that I could take care of myself. I was only twelve (and I looked about ten) but, to me, this seemed like a fun adventure.

I was such an independent-minded kid that I thought taking a solo ferry trip sounded perfectly reasonable. Even today, I don't feel like too much was being asked of me. However, it is also true that I was so naive, I simply had no idea how many things could possibly go wrong in this plan. Dad had never had a good sense of what kids are supposed to be able to handle at different ages, so he always treated us kind of like adults. He gave us jobs way too grown-up for us, but because he believed we could do it, we usually did. Despite the pressure and stress this caused, it made my brothers and me unnaturally self-confident for our ages. Everything with Dad was a trial by fire. I was used to that, though. In fact, I felt condescended to by most adults, with their age-appropriate hampering of a child's ability.

When folks saw me riding the ferry by myself, wearing a huge backpack, many asked if I was okay. I slowly began to understand that most folks were not comfortable with me being on my own. But, in all honesty, it does not take any brains to ride a ferry. You just sit there.

In England, when I passed through customs, the agent asked, "Pretty young to be traveling alone, aren't you?"

Was I? I did not know. I told the man my plan to take the train to my stepmom's apartment and then to Heathrow the next day.

"Huh!" he said. "That's going to be tough, mate. The trains are on strike." With that, he stamped my passport and looked to the next person in line.

The only kind of "strikes" I knew about were from either Little League or lighting matches, but it did not take long for me to figure out that, for some reason, the trains were not running.

I thought about that for a few minutes and figured out a new plan: I had two hundred dollars' worth of traveler's checks my Grandpa Barnes had given me for the trip. I had not spent any of it yet, so I figured I would change that into British pounds and use it to get a bus straight to the airport. I could spend the night on the airport floor, if need be, and be sure to catch my flight in the morning.

When I went to a counter to exchange the money, the lady there asked, "Are you traveling by yourself?" with an even more heightened sense of alarm than the customs agent. I tried to soothe her nerves by explaining my plan to take the bus to the airport. She looked skeptical but changed my money anyway.

As I walked toward the nearby bus station, who should come running up to me but Renée herself, wild haired and red faced, screaming, "Thaaaaaaad!"

Apparently, Dad had called to tell her I was on the way. She freaked out about the trains being on strike and drove to the ferry station to rescue me from certain European oblivion.

As she drove us to her flat, she ranted and raved about my irresponsible father. I noticed my mom and Renée talked about him in the same insanely frustrated way, so I was not surprised when, eventually, Renée told Mom about the incident, and Mom agreed putting me on that ferry alone was utterly irresponsible.

For me, the whole adventure had been an exercise in problem-solving. I never said anything about my feelings and might not have been exactly aware of what they were at the time, but I think I was a little annoyed with Mom and Renée for having so little faith in me. I was also thankful that my Grandpa Martin had given me some money. Without that, I really wouldn't have been able to make a good plan. I would have had to ask someone for money or a ride, and who knows how that could have ended. Truth is, for whatever reason, innate or environmental, I was confident and able to find solutions to issues. I would have been fine, but I guess parents are supposed to act as guardrails, not turbo chargers, for their children's ignorance.

Throughout the nineties, our family settled into the reality that Mom was a cancer *survivor*. We spoke about cancer as a thing of the past and declared it was in *remission* with the same pride my grandparents expressed when speaking of winning World War II. The cancer thing was behind Mom, just like it was behind my maternal grandmother, who had also beat cancer long ago. Meanwhile, the success of Farm Fresh To You kept Mom busier than ever, which left Freeman and me to fend for ourselves after school and during the summer in a *Lord-of-the-Flies*-worthy free-for-all nothing short of anarchy. We grew up resilient, independent, and tough as nails. We shot guns, disassembled fireworks to make explosives, hunted deer, and continued to do elaborate stunts on our bikes with zero supervision.

For six years, Mom's disease stayed in remission. That was most of Freeman's childhood, from ages nine to fifteen. For me, it was between ages twelve and eighteen, but the twins remember an entire childhood before cancer came a-knocking at all.

By the nineties, Mom had truly become a part of the Capay Valley. Her and Johnny's feuds had settled down, and she felt supported by hearing stories about Johnny's many evil doings from other Capay Valley locals who had become her friends. Like an oak tree transplanted from a pot into the earth, Mom took a while to establish herself, but by the time of her cancer remission, her roots in Capay had been established. Meanwhile, Freeman and I, who had both grown up in the Capay Valley, had even deeper roots, which stretched to places Mom knew nothing about.

A group of caring local families watched our family from a distance, witnessing with admiration our parents' honest toil on the land. As we grew, they took Freeman and me under their wings to some extent. Three men in particular—Tom, Ray, and Kenny—taught us the things they thought a proper father figure should. Through these salt-of-the-earth, hardworking, fun-living country folks, Freeman and I gained a point of view that my parents did not even know existed. From them, we learned the local tradition of blacktail deer hunting on public land. Tom, Ray, and Kenny taught us a lifestyle of hard work and hard hunting, including how to ride horses and mules and handle pack saddles, rifles, pistols, and booze.

Saturdays throughout high school, we would ride our horses to a tie-up location, then hoof it through some of California's roughest country, seeking a legal buck to shoot. Occasionally, I would actually see something. Less frequently, I would shoot at something, and even less frequently, I would kill something. Kenny taught me how to field dress a deer and shape it into a backpack as a way of getting it back to camp. At camp, we would remove the hide and cool the meat in a cotton deer bag so flies could not lay eggs in it while the meat cooled.

That crew also taught me to celebrate hard work with as many Coors Originals as possible. The next morning, we would cut the cooled deer into its primary cuts and transport it safely home, where it would become venison chops and jerky.

With fascination and admiration, Mom watched me grow into a competent hunter. After all, her (and Dad's) vision had always been to have us boys grow up with practical, real-life skills. When she watched us confidently saddle the horses, load them into the trailer, and prepare our hunting gear, she would sometimes exclaim, "What an amazing hobby!"

Immediately after returning from such a hunting expedition, I would typically pack up a van with produce boxes to deliver to Earl's Organic on Jerald Street in San Francisco: a grueling four-hour drive, all told. My teenage life was exhausting, but I enjoyed being of service to Mom and the farm. As long as I helped out, she never set limits on whatever I wanted to do for fun, so I enjoyed a level of freedom most kids and teens never knew.

Safety was never our priority, so we learned a lot of things the hard way. For instance, the first time Freeman took his new horse on a hunting trip with Danny and Kenny, he was twelve. It was the middle of the night as they crossed Cache Creek, which was running full, and the horse drifted downstream into some rocks, then fell down in the water. Freeman was briefly pinned under the beast, then managed to surface and cling onto a rock for dear life until Kenny, scanning the creek with his flashlight, saw and rescued Freeman from the water. The horse, however, ended up drowning. When Kenny delivered Freeman without his horse back to Mom, he was horrified to have to tell her the story, but Mom took the whole thing in stride. She told Kenny she appreciated him including Freeman in his weekend excursion and was just glad Freeman was okay. Then she bought Freeman another horse, Lucky Ned Pepper, and our adventures in the hills continued. Eventually, those adventures became a big part of our lives.

Throughout our childhood, Freeman and I wore Mom down with our requests for a coveted item: a Super Nintendo. Until we bought it, that thing was all we could think about, but this typical American entertainment did not turn out to be as much fun as we had thought. We soon realized that life was wasted playing video games about adventure when we had the opportunity for real-life adventures, every day. We got bucked off horses, wore the tires off go-karts, raced the delivery vans when Mom was not watching, ripped up the gravel driveway spinning donuts in farm trucks, and went through boxes of ammunition honing our marksmanship. With all that to stimulate our minds and bodies, the Nintendo quickly became something Freeman and I would only binge on when it was too dark or rainy to be outside.

Our family had a TV we kept in the closet, but using it involved rolling it out, plugging it in, and setting up bunny ear antennae that had to be endlessly adjusted to get a clear picture. Despite the hassle of setting it up, and the strict *no TV if it's light outside* rule, Freeman and I spent many hours staring at the boob tube. However, TV was not a big part of our childhood. Interestingly, our unusual childhood resulted in me being an adult who does not care much for TV but has a secret love for the once-forbidden junk food, fast food, candy, and soda pop. I am, however, blessed that I never confuse delicious junk food for delicious real food.

Around the same age, I returned home from Sunday school one day and proudly told Mom what I had learned. Apparently, the tree that grew the wood upon which Jesus was crucified felt so bad, afterward, that it grew gnarled and crooked in penance for having inadvertently participated in the crucifixion. That way, its wood could never be used for such a purpose again. I felt touched by this fact and in awe of the tree's devotion to Jesus.

Sitting at the kitchen table, Mom listened to this story while updating the calendar book that ran her life. Finally, she looked up at me and put her pencil down with a click. "Thaddeus," she said, "that's a beautiful story, but it's the most ridiculous thing I've ever heard."

The nun teaching Catechism should have known better than to bring horticulture into religion.

Mom explained that trees do not grow crooked out of "sorrow" or "penance." If plants had such mysterious motivations for growing, we could never predict a harvest or run a farm at all. Our satsuma mandarin trees did not bear fruit because they loved us or wanted to celebrate God, they bore it because we watered and fertilized them correctly and they wanted to reproduce. She assured me that farming (and forestry too, for that matter) is a science—an imperfect one, but a science, nonetheless.

It is no exaggeration to say that I was floored. Despite our ruggedness and independence in so many areas, we boys were quite innocent. As a new teenager, I still believed whatever adults told me. I also worried about getting into heaven and not going to hell, so Mom's inference that I could doubt what I learned at church was a completely new idea for me. That moment was probably the beginning of my slow but steady decline in trust for institutions.

Not long after the founding of our CSA, Mom got so into it that she instituted spring and fall Customer Appreciation Days, where the Farm Fresh To You customers came to the farm for a tour of the place and a chance to get to know all the other members. Customers would sometimes see their very first planted fields on these trips, taste the season's first strawberries right off the stem, pick a bouquet of fragrant sweet pea flowers, and maybe even spot wild turkeys.

This may have been the first time that other kids, besides our few friends or cousins, came to the farm. Their enthusiasm mystified me. They ran around with great curiosity, breathing clean country air and picking vegetables from the earth for the very first time. I did not understand their parents' excitement upon seeing our rows of vegetables, rich organic soil, and the verdant citrus orchard. This land, the only home I had ever known, was normal to me. But, over time, I gained an appreciation for our customers' love of the land, and as I got older, it made my day to watch little kids' eyes fill with wonder when they saw a dog chase a rabbit across a field or a honeybee gathering nectar. I guess I was that innocent once too, but I sure do not remember it.

At one of these gatherings, Mom set up a station where kids could plant a seed of their very own in a little pot, take it home, and watch it grow. Naturally, the children wanted to pour all the seeds into their pots, as if the seeds were a type of breakfast cereal. It took a lot of explaining to get them to comprehend the incredible amount of information contained in just one tiny seed. When Mom told them even the ancient oak trees surrounding the farm each grew from a single acorn, that really blew their minds.

On one particularly windy Customer Appreciation Day, a child spotted a hawk riding a wind current. It hovered in the air, quite close to the ground, never flapping, just drifting, pointed into the wind. The little boy probably thought the bird was saying hello to him, but it was just looking for food, as usual, with its infallible predator's eyes.

I remember watching that child stand, all alone, out in a field of tall green grass that had come alive with the wind. The grass swayed back and forth like the waves in the ocean. Flowing one way, the grass looked bright green. Flowing the other, it appeared white, depending upon which side of the grass blade lay on top. Green to white, green to white went the world, like the earth itself was two sides of a coin. In the background, trees bowed back and forth much like the grass, but more ominous.

Back when we used to earn our primary income from farmers' market sales, Capay Fruits & Vegetables had been strictly a truck farm, or a farm that loaded its weekly harvest on a truck for local sale. Farm Fresh To You, however, took us to another level. With Noah and Che off at college and Freeman and me too young (yet) to conscript into service as drivers, Mom hired a delivery service to drop the full-to-bursting boxes right at customers' doorsteps. Now the farm had graduated to being primarily a CSA, with farmers' market and wholesale sales running distant second and third places in our hearts and account books. Eventually, though, our wholesale sales of heirloom tomatoes would trump even the revenue from our CSA, but that would not happen until the last few years of Mom's life.

With these three avenues to sell our wares, one might think the farm was really moving up in the world, but "up" is a relative term when you start at bedrock like we did. The fact of the matter was that Mom, for all her brilliance at marketing, still lacked a lot of technical know-how. We had fans and friends and a growing community through the CSA, but we were still running the farm without any significant machinery, still laboriously moving irrigation pipe by hand on a daily basis, still weeding vegetables with hand implements. By the early nineties, even with our hardworking field crew and one very rickety (but prized!) John Deere 4020 tractor, we still ran the farm on about fifty hippie-kid power.

Mom's relative success as a farmer never made the work less physically demanding or reduced the hours she spent on management, but Freeman became the first of us not to have to go to middle school with his shoes duct-taped together. Mom declared herself "positively middle class" with a sense of victory that meant a lot to her. While she had been the first in her family to get a college degree, her father was a successful draftsman who had provided well for his family. The financial stability my mother's dad still provided was something she strove to provide herself. Now she was finally accomplishing this. The only trouble was that Mom was in pain all the time. She said her bones hurt. For a while, instead of going to the doctor, she talked frequently to her sister Debbie, a nurse, on the phone.

"Deb says if ibuprofen makes me feel better, it can't be cancer!" Mom often said, popping a couple of Motrin to prove how well she was.

Finally, the pain got too bad to mask with ibuprofen, and Mom hauled herself to the doctor, ready to face the music. Afterward, the family waited days for her test results, trying to act like these were normal days and this was no big deal. We had been told the cancer was in remission and expected it to stay that way.

When the phone rang, Mom was not home. I picked up. The oncologist told me to have Kathy return his call. I asked if he could tell me the results. He said no, but the awkward tone in his voice told me all I needed to know.

That afternoon, Mom spoke to the doctor in a hushed, private tone, then sat with me on the living room couch. Cuddled close and holding my hand, she bravely said, "It doesn't look good."

We hugged and cried. Freeman must have been gone because it was just the two of us. I think that day was the saddest of all of them. Doctors recommended chemo at the maximum dose, which would kill every fast-growing cell in her body. Mom was only in her late forties then, so her chances of kicking cancer again seemed good. However, after a couple of years of that, Mom had a stroke and went blind in one eye. Between the blisters, losing her hair and fingernails, the indigestion, and everything else, we could not tell after a while if she was sicker from the cancer or the chemo.

During those last few years of Mom's chemo, I brought home a college friend named Merriss, and her mother who was also fighting cancer, so they could meet Mom. As the four of us sat and talked about life and cancer and all kinds of things, I was baffled to learn that Merriss's mother had chosen to buck the western medical norms and treat her cancer with alternative methods. She knew this was risky and that the medical establishment did not support her choice. She, too, was a strong and smart woman but had resolved not to experience the terrible side effects of chemotherapy during what might be her last few years on earth. Later, Mom and I talked about how it sure didn't *look* like Merriss's mom had cancer.

Until then, I had not even realized it was possible to choose how to treat your cancer, and perhaps that was true for Mom too. In any case, Mom aggressively fought her cancer with chemotherapy, all the way up until the day the hospice nurse forced us to confront reality. In the end, both Merriss and I lost our mothers, prompting me to ponder the difficult and courageous choice each woman had made about her treatment. Even now, knowing how much Mom suffered in her last few years, I wonder what I would do if I got cancer: fight for every day on earth at the cost of my quality of life or acquiesce to the inevitable and live fewer but better days? Hopefully, I will never again be close to that decision.

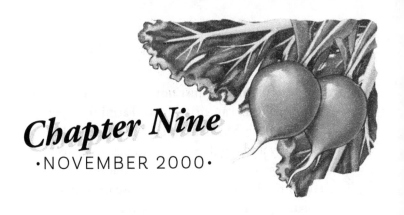

Chapter Nine
·NOVEMBER 2000·

Come November of 2000, I buried my head deeper and deeper into my studies so as to avoid having to take an incomplete in Dynamics and retake the class next semester. I did not want to stay in school a moment longer than necessary. Unlike Noah, I had not been inspired to join a fraternity, and unlike Che, I didn't experience the camaraderie that comes with military service. I just slogged through my studies, one day at a time, overwhelmed with all I had to do; meanwhile, I installed a fax machine in my rented bedroom to communicate with Chris about the farm while I did the contents sheet and the buying for Farm Fresh To You.

Even so, I tried to disconnect from the farm, emotionally, in order to embrace my chosen future as an engineer. I did not want to lose the farm, but neither did I envision myself ever managing it again. In fact, my plan was to automate my duties to the farm. Having grown up in the midst of the chaos of a farming life, I should have known better. There is nothing automatic, predictable, or easy about running an organic farm. It is just not an ordinary job, and no number of Excel spreadsheets can make it so. Farming depends so much upon the whims of both Mother Nature and the wholesale markets that trying to simplify and regulate it is a laughable project.

That year, my junior year in college, friends and lovers came and went in my life with very little sense of importance. I did not seem to be making a new world for myself at Cal Poly. After all, I was kind of a mess of a farm boy. Half hippie, half redneck, I studied thermodynamics, obsessed about lists of vegetables, and was way too comfortable talking about death. The other problem that separated me from others was the fact that I felt a strange sense of entitlement to some type of respect for what I was going through in those grief-filled years. Others, obviously and correctly, did not understand this viewpoint.

As recently as October of that year, I had been in the habit of checking in with Freeman about the farmers' market, but come November, I got too busy for that. Freeman was on his own, except that during three-day weekends, instead of having typical college-kid fun, I would drive back to the farm to see him. Back in the summer, I used to call Noah and Che once in a while, just to connect, but by November I had stopped. Things felt awkward between us. For me, there was not any anger or bitterness about all that weird funeral stuff, but there was a vague feeling that the glue that held us together had dried up.

We still knew we were brothers, still remembered being the only four animals of our species on earth, but it mattered less. Our lives together faded into the past. Without Mom, the farm was different, and life in general was immensely lonely. It had only been five months since she died, but the memory of life with Mom now seemed as distant as dinosaurs roaming earth. I had never felt so separated from where I came from and my people. Most heartbreaking of all, my family had never seemed like a memory before.

Since Mom's death, we boys had not yet made any specific plans to reunite at home. In the past, there were always plans. We had to check in with Mom, after all, and see how she was doing. In the past, Mom was always there to bring us back together, so there always used to be a sense of looking forward to our next reunion, but no more. By November, I realized how much those family gatherings used to feel like holidays for us. They had been the sparkling, transcendent moments that anchored us as we dealt with the banal stuff of life. We brothers would fight, we would drink, we would laugh. Freeman and Noah—who had both been on the wrestling team in high school—used to wrestle to amuse us all. But without Mom, there was not any urgent reason to get together anymore. As brothers, we had lost the gravity provided by the mother who always pulled us to the same place. Now, we floated around, headed in different directions.

If one of us had suggested a reunion, the others probably would have gone along with it—that is, if Che could get a vacation from the Coast Guard—but throughout that summer and fall, nobody did. I only remember studying, worrying about grades, trying to push grief from my mind, and forcing myself to get up early and stay up late to cram for exams. Then, come November, the holidays loomed on the horizon and everyone at school talked about their Thanksgiving plans. For the first time, I did not know what I would do or where I would go.

Grandma and Grandpa On-The-Hill traditionally went to Aunt Dianna's home for Thanksgiving, so that might have been the obvious place for my brothers and me to go too, but no one invited us. Maybe they just forgot us. Maybe we reminded them too much of our mother. Maybe seeing us would have made them sad. I will never know why, but that Thanksgiving, just four months after our mother's untimely death, the Barsotti side of the family made no effort to include us.

This, after we had tried to keep Mom's death a secret from the Barnes side just for them—an act that had nearly split us apart as brothers. This, after we had hidden the cards out of the funereal flower arrangements to appease our vengeful grandmother who blamed everyone named Barnes for Mom's cancer.

Freeman and I were especially shocked to realize that, without Mom, we could not count on a Barsotti family get-together. During this first holiday season, I really understood how pivotal Mom had been in holding this side of our family together. Communication with grandparents, aunts, and uncles was reciprocated when we reached out, but never initiated by them. As the holiday season approached, nobody asked about our plans, let alone invited us to anything.

The Barnes side of the family—Dad's side—did not invite us to Thanksgiving either. As kids, these grandparents, uncles, and aunts had sent us to science summer camp, brought us into family get-togethers, and shown interest in our higher education. Although our father himself was a distant figure, our relatives on the Barnes side had always been a part of our lives. That fall, though, we didn't hear from them.

None of us had ever considered, when Mom died, that along with running the farm in her stead and managing the CSA in her absence, the celebration of holidays themselves would now be entirely in our hands. While I studied for my classes that month, I tried not to be bothered by the feeling that my brothers and I were about to miss our first post-Mom holiday.

God knows none of us boys at the time could cook a turkey to save his life, so when Noah finally took the initiative and suggested we get together and have our Thanksgiving meal in a certain nice restaurant in San Francisco, Freeman and I agreed. When Che called and confirmed he would be able to make it too, I felt relieved. What was left of our family would be together for the holiday, after all. Downing a turkey sandwich, alone, in the school cafeteria, would have been so depressing. With this new perspective on the world, I, for the first time, noticed and empathized with the students who did not have a home to go back to for the holidays.

The place we went for dinner was pretty fancy for us: The Waterfront on Embarcadero Street. We were not "going out to dinner" type people as it was, but Noah thought we should treat ourselves. Even though I noticed the price of entrées was rather steep, I rationalized that paying too much for dinner would be fine if it would help us get through our first Thanksgiving without Mom. I did not realize that not all the brothers were on board with that. When Noah ordered a hundred-dollar bottle of wine, Che exploded in rage. Clearly Che had been holding himself back throughout the taxi ride to the restaurant, the process of being seated among crystal goblets and fine cutlery, the enjoyment of a waterfront view with reflections of the Bay Bridge . . . but now he just let loose. Che called Noah irresponsible and seemed disgusted by his free-spending brother and the entire dining experience.

Noah said he would pay for the wine himself. We did not have to split it or anything. But that made no difference to Che. In hindsight, Che's anger probably had nothing to do with wine or financial factors. We hadn't seen Che since July and really had no idea how he was taking Mom's death. Noah and Che had always fought one another, sometimes fiercely, over trivial things, but Che really did not seem like himself this time. Nothing Noah said or did could calm him down. That was how the meal began, so the rest of the night was basically shot. So much for our first boys-only Thanksgiving.

In the Lifetime Channel movie version of our lives, Thanksgiving would have brought us boys together again. We would have toasted Mom, shared memories, celebrated her life, and vowed to help one another pursue our own bright futures. We would have given thanks for the farm and congratulated ourselves on keeping it going for the past five months. Che would have rolled his eyes and called us crazy for even trying to keep that fucked-up little farm above water. We would have good-naturedly booed his cynicism, then Che would have sheepishly admitted he thought we were brave. What an uplifting scene that would have been.

Instead, we ate in an awkward silence punctuated by snippy comments. Grief has a lot of anger in it, but anger is not a bullet. It is more like taking double-aught buckshot from a couple hundred yards. The lead balls sink just far enough into your body to hurt you, just enough that you wish you were dead, but not deep enough to kill you.

The rest of the Thanksgiving break followed the same tone of being irritated with each other but not having anywhere else to go. Sure, we also had a few fun, drunken nights out in the city that reminded us of our special connection, but only briefly. Eventually, just like back in July, when the end of the trip came, we were all glad to head back to our own individual corners of the world.

Right after the holiday, Che returned to Puerto Rico. I did not like that he wasn't living in California with us that terrible year. It was reassuring to know two of my brothers lived within a few hours' drive, and I wished that were true of all three of them. Having Che so far away and being immersed in military culture, which was so different from the rest of our lives, kept him separate. I did not like that. Che was uncomfortable with military culture too, but the sacrifices were worth it. He got to fly airplanes for a living, which was all he ever wanted.

Mom had approved of the stability of Che's job, so she encouraged him to stay in the Coast Guard, which is the only reason Che stayed as long as he did. Same as me, Che did whatever Mom told him. Having grown up so isolated, I think we didn't really trust ourselves with decisions about "the world." Mom, who knew all about life outside the farm, observed us keenly and advised us as to the directions our adult lives would take. She did not have time or money to take us on college visits and things like that, so she simply pointed each of us in an approximate direction and told us, *This way your future lies.*

In November of 2000, we three oldest boys were all still living out the lives Mom had selected for us. None of us had stopped to question them yet. Only Freeman would be tasked with choosing his own path, and I remember thinking it would be interesting to see what became of him. I suspect the entire extended family wondered what would become of Freeman. Would he even go to college?

After Thanksgiving, our farm manager Chris called me. He had to get something off his chest: his family's first "child," their beloved dog Todd, had been murdered. At the end of last season, someone had tied the dog to a post in the irrigation canal, where it slowly drowned. I knew exactly the psychopath who had done it: our evil neighbor Johnny. But knowing Johnny was the culprit wouldn't bring the dog back, nor, for that matter, would it bring back any of the other dogs Johnny had murdered.

This was a horrible ending for what had felt like a month of pure despair. Not only was my family fractured—with all of us boys looking at each other like strangers now—but we were, once again, being sabotaged by outside forces. I didn't know how Johnny, who knew our mother had just died horribly and painfully, could do such a terrible thing to us. I *still* do not know. But, that November, I learned that just because my world stopped spinning, that did not mean anything had changed for anyone else. Crops kept growing. Cruelty was still there. Beauty existed. Evil existed. The whole world we had known with Mom was still the world we lived in. The world, I realized, does not give you a break for anything.

Chapter Ten

·LATE 1990s·

Back when my parents first bought the land, Johnny pulled one of his biggest dirty tricks on us: he planted those eucalyptus trees along the three sides of our land that bordered his, which meant they were planted under the power lines that fed electricity to our farm. This sabotage was probably more effective than he ever even planned it to be, because when those trees grew up, not only did they block the view and host the starlings that ate our peaches, they also interfered with our electricity. We could not cut the trees down, though, because they were Johnny's.

Technically, the electric company should have cut the branches back, but they did not do it often enough. At one point, the eucalyptus branches got so bad they were touching the power lines and causing electricity to arc while raining sparks down into the dry leaves and grass that lay below—a clear fire hazard. A couple of men from the electric company drove out to deal with it, but while they climbed trees and chain-sawed the branches, Johnny went out and boldly spray-painted on the hood of their blue PG&E truck: "No Trespassing."

The poor men, just trying to do their job, called their boss, who in turn called the sheriff. When the sheriff showed up, Johnny complained that the men cutting the branches had no business being on his property, which he felt justified his vandalism of their truck. When the sheriff did not agree, Johnny voiced the opinion that the Black (though he did not use that respectful word) sheriff did not know what he was talking about. Johnny's racist comments flowed throughout the heated exchange, but somehow (he was a white landowner, after all) Johnny avoided getting arrested. As soon as the branches were cut, those poor guys were glad to get the hell out of our neck of the woods, and I did not blame them.

The only good thing about having an enemy is the bonding that happens as a family unites against him, and so it was for Freeman and me, at a later date, when we finally cut those damned branches. Unlike our mother, Freeman and I had grown up in the country and understood the law of the land. If Johnny's branches grew over onto our side of the property line, they were ours to cut but his to clean up.

We were well over playing mister nice guy and trying to win our neighbor over with kindness, so when Freeman drove Terry's forklift out to where I could stand on the pallet it held up and cut the branches with a chainsaw, I holstered a .357 revolver at my waist. I knew Johnny would show up to supervise the task and make some choice comments. That was what the revolver was for.

Naturally, Johnny came roaring out of his house to meet us. Standing up above him, on that pallet, I stopped operating the chainsaw just long enough to position myself so that Johnny could clearly see the holstered revolver, front and center. He took one look at the tableau before him, paused uncharacteristically, put his hands up in the air, and said, "I don't want to cause any problems. Just stay on your side."

For once, Johnny's demeanor was docile, even compliant. I wondered how in the world my mother had let this coward of a man cause her so much grief.

"All right," I replied, adding, "Hey Johnny, when we're done with these branches, we're going to toss them on your side of the fence 'cause they're your trees."

He nodded and disappeared back into his truck.

Summers growing up, I used to work for my stepfather Terry. He paid me a fair wage, and I learned a lot from him, but I spent many fine summer days doing boring, hard labor—a hell of a way to spend the prime of your life. One summer, Freeman spent his time just being lazy. He didn't appear too concerned about making money, which seemed unlike Freeman, who was always scheming a way to come out ahead. Then, come August, my younger brother borrowed a forklift from Terry and went out on the land to pick figs off a neglected tree.

The family rule was that if you took initiative to do something like that, you got to keep the profits. For instance, Che had paid for his pilot's lessons by growing radishes and Chinese long beans. Once, when Che was tending his garden, Grandpa On-The-Hill slowed down as he drove by and yelled out the window: "You'll make more money stealing hubcaps!"

Che took this to heart and made Grandpa's hubcaps reappear for twenty dollars.

Freeman watched all this until he, too, understood the value of an opportunity. That summer, he took his figs to the farmers' market and sold them for a small fortune. In fact, he bested my entire month's wages in a single weekend. That kid was always thinking one step ahead. Another year, he worked out a deal with Terry to harvest the flowers off some lilac bushes of his. These were actually decorative plants, not technically crops, but Terry was happy to get a cut of the money Freeman made from selling the beautiful flowers. In fact, over time, Freeman developed a real sideline in flowers.

Our weekends at the Davis, Marin, and San Francisco farmers' markets ensured that should we come up with something to sell, we had ready access to consumers who might buy it, which made us always think: *What do I take for granted that city people would eat up with a spoon?* The lilacs fell into that category. Freeman was a lot like Mom in that he could think like a customer, instead of a farmer.

Case in point: I remember when Mom first got the idea to grow thin-skinned potatoes. This had never been done on any sort of scale because mainstream agriculture balked, saying this variety would be too difficult and time-consuming to harvest compared to the standard thick-skinned, durable russet potato. Mainstream ag was right. It was more expensive, but Mom understood customers would pay a premium for these delicate, gourmet potatoes you did not have to peel. She guessed the extra work and expense would pay off. She was right, and now thin-skinned potatoes are a supermarket staple. She even rightly predicted that the really small ones, called creamers, would be worth even more.

Truck farms like ours have pioneered many unusual crops: Asian pears, cherry tomatoes, baby lettuce mix, easy peel mandarins, heirloom tomatoes, and kale among them. Big growers keep an eye on small farms like ours, and when we take successful risks on unusual crops, they learn from our efforts and then invest millions into developing the crop for mass consumption. There is a kind of tragic irony in the way the agriculture industry uses these broke little farms as their ad hoc R&D department.

Terry knew that Mom had vision in a way he never could, so he trusted her and went for it with the thin-skinned potatoes too, resulting in a tidy profit. In fact, one time he told me quite seriously, "Your mom is the smartest person I've ever known."

At one point in the late nineties, Freeman and I nearly burned the farm down. We had a fort that was an old truck stashed at the edge of the property under Johnny's eucalyptus trees. This was where broken pallets were "stored" until some future date when they would be taken to the dump. The knee-high weeds that grew there dried to a tinder-like material in the summer sun.

We had learned from Noah and Che, early on, the value of Fourth of July fireworks. They were essentially gunpowder. We used to take them apart and keep the flammable firework powder and the fuses. We would then reconstruct them, wrapping the powder as tight as we could in duct tape, with the fuse hanging out, to make mini explosives. To this end, we kept a cache of Fourth of July fireworks stashed in our fort along with various other treasures, including the M-80s Dad brought us from France.

One summer day, we were bored and hanging out at the fort with a cousin and a friend. Mom had left us on the farm alone while she ran some errands. We noticed a wasp's nest wedged in among some old pallets full of dry grass. The pallets were stacked under the line of eucalyptus trees whose branches were all hanging to the ground. Now, knocking down wasp's nests was basically a sport for us. There was nothing like the rush of getting close enough to the nest to knock it down, then running as fast as possible to escape the attacking wasps. We got stung doing this all the time, but it always made for a great story and was something to do.

This particular wasp nest was pretty difficult to reach, so I had the bright idea of using some smoke bombs from our cache of explosives to smoke the wasps out. Freeman lit the smoke bomb and tossed it into the pile of old pallets where the nest was, and we waited, not knowing what to expect. To our surprise, the pile of pallets exploded into raging flames. Destroy wasp nest—check.

The flames leaped fifteen feet in the air, lapping at the eucalyptus trees. We had no idea what to do. Someone tossed two glasses of water on the huge flames, because that was all we had on hand, which of course did nothing at all. The flames leaped higher and started to burn the dry grass that ran under the line of trees, but then, as my brother, cousin, friend, and I stood there helplessly, Ricardo and a helper showed up. They ripped branches off the eucalyptus trees with their bare hands and used them to swat at the base of the fire, trying to smother it.

In the meantime, I ran to the house, picked up the phone, and dialed my grandparents On-The-Hill. When my grandfather answered, I blurted out, "Grandpa, we started a fire and can't get it out!"

There was silence for a minute until he replied, "I see that," and hung up the phone.

Ricardo and his team ended up putting the fire out, but not before my grandpa called 911. In the distance, I heard the wail of the air horn at the Esparto Volunteer Fire Department, then the fire trucks showed up. The other boys and I ended up with criminal records and were forced to receive counseling—a strange experience I will never forget.

At my counseling appointment, a soft-voiced woman asked me how many fires I had started in my life. It was a difficult question to answer, so I asked her to define what counted as "one fire." I was shocked to realize her definition included every match struck and every single flick of a lighter.

I answered as honestly as I could, saying simply, "Thousands?"

Her eyes bugged open! Looking back, I have to laugh at the ignorance of that woman, with her suburban lifestyle expectations, who was unfairly tasked by the State of California with "analyzing" a kid whose culture she knew nothing about. She did not know my parents or enough about the typical lifestyle of a farm kid to counsel or pass judgment on me. Nonetheless, she concluded that I habitually started fires because I was angry about my parents' divorce and wanted attention. I was baffled by this assessment. We had been trying an innovative new method of eliminating wasps. That was all. In my own final analysis, my big mistake was not trusting Ricardo to take care of it. In calling Grandpa, I had summoned "the authorities," whom my family had always avoided at all costs. Now, I understood why: educated idiots and authority are a toxic combination.

In high school, I was a good student despite my atrocious spelling and handwriting, but I really excelled at working with my hands. I was the first on our farm to weld, which says a lot about how ill-equipped my parents were. After learning to weld, I became interested in the precision required in the art of woodworking. I enjoyed it. I remember making a walnut jewelry box with a drawer that pulled out and a top that opened. It had dovetail joints made of oak, fitted perfectly so there were no gaps. The front of the box showcased the grain, and in that part of it I cut a little place for a drawer.

"What you could have done here," Mom remarked upon seeing my work, "was to save the piece of wood you cut out and use it to make the drawer. That way the grain in the box and the door would line up perfectly."

I did not take her suggestion as criticism at all. I loved how Mom appreciated the piece for what it was but didn't give me a pass. She expected me to care about making it the best I could. I did care. I wanted to see my work and myself through her eyes. With one small comment, she gave me that. I love that memory of her.

When we boys were little, Dad used to bring home random things he got for free or traded for produce, like a busted bicycle or a broken go-kart. I always found a way to tinker around and make these things work with hose clamps or duct tape or some such amateur rigging. Later, when I learned about welding, I realized it was very strange that, for a decades, we did not have a welder or torch on the premises. This is standard equipment on a farm!

None of my brothers had ever really excelled at fabrication, so this skill was yet another thing that made me an essential part of the farm. I liked it. In high school, I learned to weld with arc, MIG, and gas setups. I could use a chop saw and horizontal band saw to cut metal. I could polish off bad welds and rust with a grinder. I could use an oxyacetylene torch to heat metal for bending with a rosebud, or I would cut it with a torch. I became comfortable with a drill press and a lathe too. Slowly, over time, we collected these valuable tools in an ever-growing shop building on the farm. Neither of my overeducated parents could build or repair things worth a damn, and over time, I came to realize how weird this was for a farm family. We were lucky that Terry came along when Dad left because he tutored me on those essential skills using his own farm-equipped shop.

Once Terry joined the family in the early nineties, January on the farm became dedicated to refurbishing machinery. It rained too much at that time of year to do much else. Every winter, he would select a machine—a tractor, a forklift, a disk—and completely take it apart. Every nut and every bolt came off. He would clean, inspect, and replace the worn parts and lubricate every piece, then put the whole thing back together again. It seemed like a miracle to me that when he put it back together, it started right up! The first time I saw him do that, I rightly thought he was a wizard.

When I was a teen and worked for Terry during the summers, he saw my potential but was not the type to build up a guy's confidence. He never let on that I had a decent working brain, so I did not realize it. Then, one day, Terry and a couple of his guys were sitting around trying to figure out how to retrofit a fertilizer box so that instead of broadcasting fertilizer, it would put down bands of it where the plants were growing. When I joined the group, I solved the problem then and there. It was easy.

Arrogantly, I laughed at them, asking, "Really? You couldn't figure that out?"

Everyone looked a bit uncomfortable until Terry smacked me down with, "Yeah, well, that's why we keep you around, isn't it?"

I got the message: *You're clever, okay? Now shut up about it.*

This was all part of learning how to straddle the space I occupied between rural American and progressive foodie. In the world of manual labor, intelligence was a secret weapon that you learned to use carefully. So-called intelligence was often trumped by experience, so it made sense to turn to the most experienced person around before the "smart guy." Occasionally, though, when the stars align perfectly, intellect will take down a mountain of experience and redefine how a job is done, forever. More often than not, though, being the smart guy puts a target on your back. If I learned one thing in public school, it was the value of keeping the target off my back, so I watched my smartass comments from then on.

Another time, Terry and Mom rented a bin dumper. This is a really handy machine for dumping bins of potatoes into the wash line, and it is not the type of thing you can go buy off the shelf. If you can find one, they are expensive, so Terry told me, "Before we return that machine, duplicate it."

I had no idea such a thought might even cross through a person's head, but I did as told. I walked around the thing a few times, took note as to how the hydraulic system worked, measured every piece of metal, sketched a drawing of it, and made a list of the materials I would need.

I used my drawing, got to welding, and damn if I did not duplicate the machine. It was a very empowering moment! My creation didn't come close to Terry's next-level machine-making skills, but I felt proud of it. That is, until I saw Terry's homemade cucumber harvesting machine. I could not believe he had invented and built that whole thing from scratch, but that was pure Terry.

When Terry was a young man, his farm mainly raised cucumbers for seed. In this industry, seed-growing companies work out the genetics of the best cucumbers and tell the farmer, *We want this male bred with this female for a perfect hybrid.* Farmers grow the fruit solely to extract the seed from it, then sell the seeds right back to the seed company. To do this, a guy like Terry will plant twenty acres of the female interspersed with a row of male plants between every six rows. When the plants flower, he makes sure there are plenty of bees in the field to facilitate pollination. Then, at just the right time, he will mow down the male plants and harvest the females.

The most expensive thing about any farm in a capital-rich economy is the manual labor. Machines are great for tilling and prepping the soil, but harvesting requires the fruits to be separated from their vines. Come harvest season, the labor bills really add up. In Terry's case, however, it did not matter if the cucumbers got bruised since he only needed the seeds. So he invented an entire motorized machine to harvest his cucumbers. It had lights, an engine, hydraulics, the works. He painted it blue, and it looked like the most eccentric vehicle ever.

It had a cutter on the front that cut the plants at the base, severing the roots. A chain then scooped the plants out of the soil and deposited them on a conveyor belt made of rolling cylinders. The torn-up plant stems would then slip through the cracks between the rollers while the cucumbers stayed on top, and finally the cucumbers landed in a catch-all bin. Terry built an extra feature into the machine too: with a flip of a switch, the conveyor belt could be reversed. This was useful for when the plants clogged the machine. You just reversed the direction a couple of times, the clog came out, and you were on your way again.

Funny thing about Terry's machine: I do not know if he was the first person to invent this machine or not, but today, these machines are in common use on cucumber seed farms. Just like the way larger farms often copy the successful fruit and vegetable choices of more ad-venturous small farms, the industry has no shame in copying self-fab-ricated machines. To this day, Terry swears that while he may not have been the first person to invent a cucumber harvesting machine, the all-important reversal switch was definitely his innovation. Today, that feature is a standard part of cucumber harvesting machines the world over.

In the summers, when I worked the land for Terry, I learned a lot about how real farmers with proper equipment do things. So, for me, the farm was not just a slog of hard labor like it had been for Noah and Che.

The older brothers grew up in abject poverty with Dad for a male role model and bicycles for transportation, while Freeman and I grew up in only near poverty, even seeing glimpses of a middle-class lifestyle, with Terry for a role model and trucks and horses for transportation. Like our older brothers, we also did our share of all-night delivery driv-ing, packing produce boxes, and manning the farmers' market stand, which was exhausting, but not back-breaking labor for us. In fact, for Freeman and me, life on the farm was a full one that produced many fond memories.

A proficient farmer, Terry conveyed to me a wealth of knowledge I still use today. By contrast, Noah's friends refused to come over after school because they knew they would be recruited to move sprinkler pipe. Perhaps that explains why, after Mom's death, Noah eagerly returned to his life in San Francisco, while I was the one who stayed on the farm, tried to save it, and worked things out with the IRS and the CCOF.

The minute I received my driver's license, even though I had barely driven on the highway yet, I was already as overconfident behind the wheel as I had been crossing the English Channel alone on that ferry. Mom used to do too many of the deliveries herself, and she needed a break. Now that I was sixteen, it was time for me to help her. When she told me what I had to do, I was excited for the big adventure but also scared shitless. Many cultures have their coming-of-age rituals, and for our farm, that transition into manhood was delivering produce in the big city, all alone.

Sitting at the kitchen table, her face sunburned from a day in the field, her hands calloused from planting seedlings, Mom explained the route. The first drop was in Marin. I was to take the 505 South to 80 West to Route 37 South, which turns into 101 South, take some exit there, turn left, right, right again, then left, and find a certain truck parked outside a warehouse. The combination on the truck was 3276 (for some reason, I still remember it). I was to open the truck's sliding door, put the delivery inside, and close it again.

"Don't forget to leave a copy of the bill of lading!" she admonished.

The second stop was in Oakland, so I was to get back onto 101 South, take 580 East, which goes over the bay and connects to Highway 80 West, which turns into 101 South. I was to take a certain exit, turn left on a certain street, right on another street, into a sketchy looking industrial area . . . These instructions went on and on as I scribbled them down in excruciating detail.

I gathered up the notes I had jotted down, and, on the back of an envelope, Mom drew the path of a particularly confusing exit onto

Bayshore Boulevard in San Francisco. Thus armed, off I drove. Mom herself had fallen asleep at the wheel a couple of times on these long, exhausting trips, so that added to my nervousness. There were five stops total, one van filled with produce, no cell phone, no GPS, no road map, no credit card. Nothing but a determination to remain attentive and not disappoint Mom. Trying to stay calm, I distinctly remember giving myself a pep talk about just focusing on one stop at a time, not the whole route. The assignment was overwhelming, and I wished someone would come with me that first time to give me some on-the-job-training, but the whole point of me doing this was the fact that Mom would not need to, so I was, by necessity, on my own.

Unfortunately, I succeeded one hundred percent with the deliveries that day, so this arduous semiweekly task became my new job. File that under "no good deed goes unpunished," I guess. I would do it Wednesday after school and then again Sunday after having spent the weekend deer hunting. I must have been a glutton for punishment, but I always liked the feeling of completing meaningful tasks.

Some of my success doing the deliveries was based on a lesson learned once from Che when he was in the Coast Guard, and I was a teen. He came home for a visit and helped me make a delivery run to a new wholesaler on our list. Naturally, we got lost along the way, so Che stopped at a gas station and bought a road map. (This was way before smart phones, kids.)

"Can you believe this?" he asked, stabbing the map with his finger. "Can you believe Mom and Dad never so much as gave us a single fucking map to find our way to all those deliveries? They just scribbled down directions on the back of an envelope! We'd get lost for hours, driving around like idiots!" He was genuinely—and pretty legitimately—pissed off about this.

This had happened to me, too, of course, many times, but somehow it never occurred to me before that moment that store-bought maps existed and could be used to find the way to very specific locations. I marveled out loud at the realization.

"I know!" he said. "Me either! It took until I joined the Coast Guard and learned how normal people do things. Step one: buy a fucking map!"

My mind was duly blown by this conversation. This was the way our family ran, though. It was not always efficient, and we seldom had the right tools for the job, but we were always free to be ourselves and try to do whatever it was we wanted to do.

The hardest part of doing deliveries was the danger of falling asleep at the wheel. Our old van had no air conditioning and just a scratchy radio, so even without the exhaustion, the heat alone could put me to sleep as I drove the return trip north from cool San Francisco and into the searing heat of Capay Valley. I remember how I used to get so tired, I would play games with myself, like closing my eyes to the count of three while driving. That finally made me realize I needed to pull over and take a catnap, so I eventually learned to stop in certain parking lots along the way. I would crawl onto the flattened produce boxes in the back of the smelly van and drop into slumber for ten to fifteen minutes. That made all the difference and surely saved my life many times.

Besides driving, the job entailed hand-loading and unloading innumerable boxes, which added to the exhaustion but was a great way to wake up. I also enjoyed getting to know all the rough and quirky personalities at the docks and warehouses. I did not realize this until much later, but, no doubt, encountering these rough guys was far less pleasant for her than me, so it was just as well I took over the delivery driving.

Just after getting my driver's license, I became aware of a vote that would take place in our community to approve or deny a permit for a local gravel mine. By age sixteen, I was a Capay Valley young man through and through and understood the complexity of this issue. Many locals, my friends, viewed the mine as part of this region's economic lifeblood. It provided both jobs and useful aggregate for construction. On the other hand, I also understood that the gravel mine was an open sore on the land that would never heal, could easily be contaminated, and would change the character of Cache Creek forever. Team Rural America wanted the mine, but my father Martin and his environmentalist friends in Davis did not. Sitting in the middle of this issue were all the businesses in the community that just wanted to get along with everyone.

Dad was in California at the time, working on his magazine, *The Flatlander*, and he devoted an entire issue to fighting the mine. Its articles went so far as to demonize anyone in favor of the gravel mine. One day, after a farmers' market, Dad and I stopped by the local gas station, which was owned by an acquaintance of ours named Paul. After filling up with gas, Dad asked Paul for permission to leave a stack of *The Flatlanders* at the gas station, but Paul, visibly uncomfortable with the request, said no. He reminded my father that, as a local business that served everyone, he had to stay neutral on this contentious community issue.

To my great embarrassment, Dad bullied him, presenting the ultimatum that Paul accept the stack of *Flatlanders*, or he would take his business elsewhere in the future. Paul acquiesced, after which Dad threw the pile of propaganda on the counter and stormed out.

In my heart, I tended to agree with Dad that the mine was not good for the environment, but I also understood the other point of view. After all, that gravel mine helped build our local roads. In fact, our organic farm, with its daily harvests and frequent delivery runs, used those roads more than most. Dad forcing Paul to distribute his magazine really irked me. As usual, Dad only saw his side of the issue. You just cannot live that way in Capay Valley if you want to get along. Furthermore, I could count a dozen of Paul's customers—probably more profitable customers than we—who I knew would absolutely flip when they saw that *Flatlander* at the gas station. The entire encounter made me sick to my stomach. I felt ashamed of my father and resolved to redeem my family's good name as cooperative members of the community.

The next day, I stopped by Paul's. *The Flatlanders* were still there.

I said, "Hey Paul, you don't need to have these here," and tossed the entire stack into a trash can, adding, "Sorry about that!"

I could see relief flow over Paul's face when he grabbed my hand and shook it sternly, saying, "Thank you so much, Thad."

The proposition passed, and the gravel mine got the permit they needed to go deep into the water table to mine its invaluable aggregate. I was too young to vote, but democracy won out. Either way, I was relieved that I had done the right thing with those *Flatlanders*.

Terry and Johnny were very similar: both products of the same generation, both local good old boys. Neither trusted the government. They used the exact same Allis Chalmers tractor, both were good farmers, both understood equipment, and both knew how to be conniving. Johnny farmed conventionally, trusting the local chemical salesmen to steer him straight, then cheated government subsidy programs every way he could. However, Terry's distrust of the government and outsiders extended to the agriculture industry itself.

Organic farming, for Terry, came not from a place of idealism but rather practicality. Terry was from a farming family that predated all the chemical tools, so in his childhood, there had been only one way to farm. When he started farming on his own, as an adult, he did it conventionally at first, with synthetic inputs, like everyone else; however, by the time Terry came into my life, he had long ago switched back to organic farming. He had simply realized going chemical-free made more sense. Also, refraining from taking the "advice" of brand-name fertilizer and chemical companies left more profits for him.

Terry knew how to get things done. He taught me to weld, fabricate equipment, cut metal with a torch, shoot rifles, and reload ammunition. He passed on some of what he knew to me, but there was a lot he knew that just was not accepted any longer. For instance, when he was a kid, in Boy Scouts, they taught him how to make a duck pond by blowing up a fertilizer bomb where you wanted the pond. Back then, bomb-making materials such as fertilizer and diesel were readily available, and the relevant skills were no secret. Not so much today!

Terry also had the ability to talk big . . . bigger than he was willing to act on. With Johnny, Terry saw a man who had it coming, so one day he told me he had come up with a "foolproof" plan to end John-ny's reign of terror. Problem was, it involved murder, and the murderer was to be me.

"Listen, Thad," Terry told me, out in the shop after Johnny had once again reduced my mother to tears. "Here's all you have to do . . . Go into town and steal a car."

Terry's voice was calm; his manner, unhurried. He spoke as if he had given this matter a good deal of thought, and he presented his solution as elegant, practical, and inevitable. As he spoke, I was cleaning up the shop but quickly stopped and gave him my undivided attention.

"Take that single-shot twelve gauge with you. Saw the barrel off with the chop saw, so it's easy to maneuver. Load it with a round of double-aught buck shot," Terry said. He looked at me directly. If he was kidding, there was not an ounce of it in his face.

"What you do," he added, "is drive the stolen car down by the creek, back and forth, back and forth, where you can see the house. You know Johnny. He will come out, confront you, and kick you off his property.

"When he does," Terry said, still looking me in the eyes, "shoot him in the face."

I looked at Terry with disbelief, eyebrows raised, thinking, *is this really happening?* Bad as Johnny was, and as much as I hated him, I was no murderer. This was a side of Terry I had not seen before, so, curious as to the deep inner workings of this man my mother had married, I nodded to hear how his idea would end. Terry continued.

"Leave Johnny there, then take and get rid of the vehicle," Terry said. "Take it somewhere and abandon it on the side of the road where you can walk back to your truck on a path where nobody will see you. Remove everything you are wearing. In fact, wear shoes that are too big in case you leave footprints. Put all those clothes in a dumpster. In the welding shop, melt down the gun with a torch and toss it in the creek. You'll never get caught."

I looked at the oxygen and acetylene tanks that connected to the torch and imagined melting that shotgun down to a glowing, bright-orange heap of melted metal with a rosebud torch. His plan was good, but besides the murder part, stealing a car also hung me up. Even if I wanted to do this, the thought of stealing a car was even more foreign to me than blasting Johnny with a shotgun. I supposed, though, I could figure it out, and this was an interesting realization: I probably could get away with murder. Thankfully, wired into my existence was a total lack of desire to murder anybody. Johnny was an asshole who certainly had it coming. I would not have minded if someone had murdered him, but it was not going to be me.

Terry followed up a few moments later, adding, "Even if they do catch you, you're a kid. Just start crying and say, 'He was being mean to my mommy! I had to protect her!' You'll get away with it."

I chuckled at the thought of me in a court of law, acting like some scared baby to a judge and jury. No, I never considered murdering Johnny. My moral compass was stronger than that, although I fervently wished Johnny's empty heart would give out as soon as possible.

Years later, I recalled that story to Terry, laughing and saying, "Hey, remember when you gave me a game plan to murder Johnny?"

Terry denied it, though. Maybe he forgot. Maybe it never happened.

We did end up getting a certain type of revenge on Johnny, though. As he got older, the old man's aggression calmed a bit, but as we got older too, our willingness to push Johnny's buttons grew a bit. Country folks take their driveways very seriously, and Johnny was no exception. My parents chose to build our driveway right next to where Johnny's driveway met the highway, in essence creating a shared driveway entrance off the highway, separated by an imaginary property line: one driveway headed perpendicular off the highway to Johnny's house, and the other ran parallel to the highway before curving to our house.

In high school, Freeman and Danny used to drive home for lunch sometimes in Danny's beat-up white Toyota Corolla, so when Danny would exit off the highway, he would do it early, to start on Johnny's side of the gravel driveway and then pull the emergency break, locking the back tires up to leave a huge skid mark in the gravel just long enough to only be on Johnny's side. This turned into a habit. So, before long, Johnny took his backhoe and made a little ditch on the imaginary property line to prevent the skid marks. This showed us we were getting to him, and it made the sport even more fun. Danny could drive, and this ditch was no deterrent. In fact, the driveway was now an obstacle course where he made skid marks all over Johnny's side of the drive, some even right over the top of the little ditch. Then Johnny put an orange traffic cone out. That was fun too. A target! Danny would hit the driveway and pull the emergency brake on to lock the back tires up so the car would fish tail, the back tires knocking the cone over—ten points!

One day Johnny changed the cone up and replaced it with one of the tall, skinny road cones. This was cool, so Danny hit this cone with even more speed . . . Thump! Danny and Freeman looked at each other. Something was not right. They looked in the rear-view mirror, and the cone was lying down in such a way they could see that Johnny had first driven a metal T-post into the ground before hiding it with the cone! By the time Freeman and Danny finished eating lunch and headed back to school, Johnny had stood the cone up again and placed the mudflap that was ripped off Danny's car on top as a trophy. Johnny got some points back on that one.

When I was in high school, Mom discovered a French carrot called the Nantes carrot, which is so high in sugar it practically tastes like a crunchy fruit instead of a root. No commercial farm wants anything to do with it, of course. The tops are weak and susceptible to powdery mildew, and the carrots snap into pieces if they're tossed too much during the harvest, packing, or transportation processes. We had to dedicate extra labor and extra packaging to bring these high-sugar carrots to market, so we charged quite a bit to make up for all that. It didn't matter, though. One taste, and people would pay anything. They had to amaze their friends at dinner parties with this magical carrot. They had to get their kids to love their veggies by serving them this mind-blowing thing. One CSA customer even told me about how her family rations the bunch of carrots in the kitchen, when they arrive, splitting them evenly among each member of the family, including the dog! It's amazing the power a single carrot, grown right, can have over human behavior.

To sell them, Freeman and I made a giant display by piling the carrots, with their green leafy tops, in a huge heap, like a Bugs Bunny fantasy scene. I cut carrots up into bite-sized pieces and hawked the free samples, saying "Try these carrots! They're the best in the world! But watch out! If you eat one, you'll never be able to stop!"

When people tried the samples, I made sure everyone around saw their reactions.

One guy crunched down on a carrot and said, "Holy shit, that's a good carrot!"

Then, everybody wanted one. People at the farmers' market saw the crowd gathering, and that made more people flock to the scene in pure pandemonium.

While I drew people in with the free samples and friendly banter, Freeman, back in the booth, sold carrots and kept restocking like crazy to keep that pile looking high and lush and bright orange and green. The color, the scent, the sense of the rarity of this very special vegetable—it all contributed to creating a short-lived craze for carrots. We could be quite a team, Freeman and I.

I left for college in 1998, when we still used house phones to communicate. My mother died without ever feeling the need for a more up-to-date form of communication; however, Dad, with his obsession with being "on the cutting edge," avidly kept up with the latest technology. He made sure we boys got laptop computers and email accounts as early as possible. So, my first year in college, I received a message from Freeman's new email address. As I read it, I became utterly amazed at how Freeman's ability to write had exploded. This was such a comprehensive and thoughtful email with no spelling or grammatical errors at all! It wasn't until the bottom of the email, where I read, "Love, Mom," that I realized Mom had borrowed Freeman's email account to send the message.

While Mom was not on the cutting edge of internet technology, she was no dummy and gladly accepted an offer from a customer of hers who bartered a deal to exchange vegetables for a website: www.farmfreshtoyou.com. That guy did such a good job of categorizing Mom's recipes by their dominant vegetables that the site became one of the top recipe sites in the world for a while! We still chuckle about how clueless we were back then. Compliments came in from around the world on our recipe website, and we never even considered exploring that strength. The early 2000s would have been a smart time to invest a little effort into that business strategy.

Chapter Eleven

·DECEMBER 2000·

Driving in the rain from Cal Poly up to the farm, I thought about talking to Mom, and the thought gave me a phenomenal rush of pleasure. I viscerally felt how talking to her about my day was going to make everything okay. I remembered how she would give me advice on dealing with my toughest classes and interpersonal problems. That day, when I was driving, I had had a bad day, the rain was not helping my mood, and the thought entered my mind: *Oh, I can talk to Mom! That'll really feel good, right now!* I felt so good on a deep soul level, knowing that just hearing my mother's voice would jolt me out of my misery. Then, I remembered she was dead.

Not only did the sudden remembrance of her death about six months prior plunge me into an ever-deeper sadness, but I realized that every single time my brain did this to me I would have this experience again. Mom was not there for me that day, and, I somehow finally realized, she would *never be again*. The whole experience, from anticipation to realization, must have lasted a split second, but a million and one emotions crossed through my heart in that time.

When the end of 2000 rolled around, I had done the paperwork to turn our farm into "Capay Incorporated," but to the public we would be "Capay Organic" and "Farm Fresh To You." By this time, being organic was so much a part of who we were that I figured replacing "Capay Fruits & Vegetables" with "Capay Organic" made sense. This was yet another thing that took me away from my studies. Mom had not ever thought of the farm as anything but her way of life, and she was ignorant to the potential benefits of creating a legal entity separate from herself. For Mom, the farm *was* her, and she and the farm would share the same fate, whatever that may be.

My brothers appreciated all the work I did to make Capay Inc. happen so that the farm could one day, maybe, make some money, but at that time, it was still nothing more than a side hustle for us. As for me, I took an incomplete in Dynamics and cringed when I saw I had earned a 2.54 GPA for the quarter. If I kept that up, my GPA for the year would erode to below 3.5 in a hurry. If Mom were alive, she would have berated me for it. I could hear her voice reminding me in a loving but get-your-shit-together tone: "Thaddeus, in our family, we get As and Bs." This memory helped me set a personal goal for myself of a 3.5 GPA. I reasoned that scoring under three meant I was not paying enough attention to school. Too close to four, though, would mean I was paying too much attention to school and not enough to life in general.

After my brothers' and my lackluster Thanksgiving, I did not have high hopes for Christmas. Still, though, we boys had never yet spent a Christmas apart, and this was certainly not the year to start. Another fancy dinner in San Francisco was definitely not the way to go, though. On the farm, we always used to do things Mom's way, but now that Chris and his family were living in the house, we could not use it, so even a little thing like a family gathering was no longer easy to pull off.

Every location besides our family home felt wrong and strange.

That month, Che declared what this family needed was a total paradigm shift. He had tried and failed to relate to Noah's new way of life; so, this time, he suggested we all try to relate to his in Puerto Rico. The world of the Coast Guard was mysterious to me, and I had always thought it would stay that way. Excited to learn all about my brother's life, I readily agreed.

When Freeman, Noah, and I arrived in San Juan on Christmas Day, Che picked us up at the airport and whisked us off to a barbecue his friends were hosting on the beach. Blackened local fish, lobster, steaks, the works: it was an amazing gathering with great folks, very casual, very fun, no hundred-dollar bottles of wine in sight, but plenty of beer. Lush vegetation surrounded us, and beautiful cliffs loomed in the distance. Before the sun set into the perfectly warm tropical night, I marveled at the ocean's incredible turquoise blue. It felt strange to me that this foreign place was the home of Che, a brother to whom I felt so close.

Ironically, I had always, in a way, felt bad for Che with the life he chose. The best path toward his lifelong dream of flying airplanes seemed to be accepting admission into the US Coast Guard Academy and heading down the path of becoming an officer in the military. He did not know it at the time, but with this decision he had exchanged what could have been four years at a university, exploring the limits of life, for four years of strict boot camp. At any rate, with Mom's blessing and encouragement, he accepted. But being in the military, kowtowing to superiors, and being subject to all that regimentation was hell for him. We really were not raised to follow orders except in the sense of, "Figure out how to do this impossible task, do it somehow, and let me know when it's done."

I now know that while I complain that it took all my college years for me to learn to be social, Che, who went through college in the Coast Guard Academy, had an even worse time with this challenge. He seemed to have emerged from that trial by fire with a lot of social skills, though, because, by December of 2000 in Puerto Rico, he had quite a fun scene around him.

True to form, my brothers and I and this whole crowd of friendly strangers drank until things got crazy. The barbecue became a full-on bonfire. We stripped down to shorts and danced around the fire like lunatics. Che's friend became the real life of the party when she entertained us with a topless rendition of a cover song. The fire's glow reflected off her tanned skin like something in a priceless Renaissance painting. All this made me feel like I was living someone else's incredibly free and beautiful and lucky life. This never would have happened back in Yolo County, that's for sure. It struck me that this was the type of life my young, hippie parents might have lived when they were my age. I had never before thought of my mother living this way—young and carefree.

I do not know what I expected when I got on that plane Christmas morning, but it wasn't this. I supposed Che's Christmas would have some measure of regimentation, reserve, and traditional military protocol. I must have thought that the life Che led—which had caused him to despise the very concept of fancy restaurants and expensive wines—was severe, conservative, and penny pinching. No, indeed. I guess I did not know my brother as well as I thought. While he worked hard and paid more attention to rules than I ever had, he had also learned to turn it all off and let loose when he wasn't on duty.

Out in Puerto Rico, Che lived more Yolo County than Yolo County itself, only with mostly good weather and glorious beaches. Sure, Che had to toe the line when he went to work each day and be mister perfect when he flew planes, but it was here that I learned it was routine in military culture to drink and live life to the max when off duty. I heartily approved.

I got into a Jeep that night with a woman from the bonfire who was far too drunk to drive. Still in my careless phase that Christmas, I was a bit crazed, doing my share of dangerous driving and thoughtless living. I was in that whatever-happens-happens phase of grief, where—despite the fact that I was working my ass off for the farm while going to college—I acted like I did not care much if I lived or died.

We drove way too fast going down a highway that had been recently wetted with a warm tropical rain, and her vehicle went into a skid, then spun . . . once, twice, I do not know how many more times, doing 360s down the middle of the highway. Drunkenly, from the passenger seat, I watched telephone poles swooshing by, one after the other after the other after the other. My head spun inside the car while the world itself spun outside. We went dead silent for what felt like hours but was actually seconds, watching those telephone poles swoosh, swoosh, swoosh past us. We didn't so much surrender to fate as just hold our breath in disbelief.

Next thing I knew, the Jeep planted itself in a ditch, right between two telephone poles. We looked at each other, then at the unharmed vehicle, and just laughed our asses off. We could have been dead. We could have been maimed. Worse yet, we could have brought harm to someone else. But all we were, at this point, was a little dizzy. We laughed and laughed like the fact that we did not die that night was the funniest thing in the world.

Somehow, we made it back to the bonfire on the beach, where a light sprinkle soon turned into a downpour. Nobody gave a damn about the rain. We just pounded more beers, took shots of rum, stoked the fire to keep it blazing, and goofed around on the beach. I did not plan to repeat the careless drunk driving bit, but aside from that, this was my brothers and me at our best—getting wild, cutting loose, having fun, and being those no-boundaries kids we had been raised to be.

We were out until the sun woke up the horizon. We watched the sky turn pink, then purple, then orange, as the sun's wobbling orb rose above the water like liquid gold. Finally exhausted, one by one, Freeman, Noah, Che, and I face-planted into the sand to sleep off our truly crazy Christmas beneath the fan-like leaves of coconut palms.

Over the course of that week, Che took us snorkeling, laughed as we attempted to surf, kept us plied with Puerto Rican rum, and let us sleep in until eleven every morning before taking us on some great, new adventure. He even took me flying in his new airplane, a Piper Cherokee. Looking down on the island, the jungle, and the ocean, we zipped through the sky, and I could not believe my luck to experience this, nor could I believe that Che owned an airplane. What a life! Che had made it just about as far from the farm where we grew up as he could possibly go—not just distance-wise, but psychologically too. He was not bound to the earth in any way.

Che had been the first one of the twins out of the womb. He emerged just before midnight. Noah came a few minutes after midnight, so the twins had consecutive birthdays. Che always seemed to have taken his status as eldest-by-a-few-minutes to heart. He had always been the kind, responsible, take-charge brother. In our family, Noah was the wild one, Freeman was the kid, I was whatever I am, but Che was always the big brother. The reliable one. The rock.

Getting off the farm had always been Che's driving force. Being secluded on that twenty-acre patch left Che to focus on the airplanes flying overhead, all going somewhere else. Sure, that does not paint the farm in a very good light, but at least the scarcity of cash and isolation gave Che a focus early on. As for me, I was still exploring life's possibilities. I had no idea where life would take me, really. I had not yet met my life partner, nor had I committed to any particular profession.

I was still interested in keeping the farm alive, partially for sentimental reasons and partly because I had a hunch we could make something of it. I thought maybe we could keep the farm and the memories of our childhood and our dear mother and do something else on the land. At the time, I never dreamed of dedicating my life to the farm. At that point, I could not imagine we would one day turn those twenty acres of "hippie heaven" into the largest CSA in the country, maybe the world. I never dreamed the bet we made on the farm would provide careers for us and that ultimately the farm would provide for our kids in a way it never had done for us. If anyone had told me that was to be the fate of me, my family, and that cursed little farm, I would have snickered and considered a polite rebuttal to the insult. None of that seemed possible in the year 2000.

Ever since Mom's death, I had been clinging to every aspect of my life by my fingernails, trying not to let the little I could claim as my own slip through my hands. I gripped my share of the newly formed and valueless Capay Inc. with white knuckles. That year, my future felt as tissue thin and delicate as an oak leaf in the fall. Yet here was Che, living a full, fascinating, completely independent life. Seeing that gave me hope and made me feel like, *Yeah, man! I can do it! I can build a life of my own, just like Che!* I did not know how or when or where this would happen, but I fed off Che's confidence, just like I used to as a child. Being around him made me feel like anything was possible.

We four brothers had certainly been drunk together before, but not like this, for days on end. It felt necessary and cathartic, though. We were not sensitive souls, us boys. We didn't have a tradition of talking about our feelings and emotions. We cursed each other. We shouted. We punched. Sometimes we also grudgingly apologized. No matter what, though, we always reunited in brotherhood. Years of our mother telling us to always stick together, no matter what, left it ingrained in our beings to resolve conflicts even when we hated each other. Despite having hippies for parents, we are not a touchy-feely bunch. Being together like this, for a whole week, with Mom nowhere in sight, was, I think, secretly hard but healing for all of us. Whenever something good happened, I wanted to call Mom up and tell her.

In a way, that Christmas, we talked about how we all missed Mom, but the way we were able to do it without crying was to bitch about how unfair it was that she died so young at just fifty-one. She never got to see any of us get married or hold a single grandchild. Nobody said it, but we all missed Mom that week more than we could handle.

We did not want to fall into some maudlin, depressing conversation about how much Mom would have loved this or that and how we wished we could show her the beautiful beaches and the sea from the air. Talking about it would have only brought us down, so we partied. And partied. And partied some more. By New Year's Eve, I felt positively nauseated, but the party could not stop because we wouldn't have known what to do with each other without that common activity.

On New Year's Eve, Che's friends came over to Che's house, where we were all staying, and insisted on a game of quarters. We got drunk, naturally. A lot of that night is a blur. I do remember that at one point, I fell down and someone covered me in booze, like a baptism.

Later, we enjoyed the glorious sounds of shattering glass as we launched beer bottles off the balcony to smash on the patio below. Then, someone threw Che's plastic lawn furniture and smashed it too. The drunken trend was one of destruction and explosion, which seemed fitting somehow. For Noah, Freeman, and me, this was our last night in Puerto Rico and the end of something special.

In the midst of the party, I wandered into the TV room to find Freeman and Noah wrestling. It all started very innocently, but things escalated out of control. Che soon joined the melee, on Freeman's side, taking the opportunity to deliver some of his childhood rage back to his fraternal twin.

These were no friendly pushes and jabs. I watched, amused by the turn of events, as Noah fought to defend himself from the other two. A music stand got knocked down in the tussle and then Che bent it around Noah's neck. Che tried to connect each end of the music stand together around Noah's neck, while Noah resisted with his hands, to make sure he could still breathe. At this point, being a bystander was no longer possible. Two people were fighting one of my brothers, and he was losing. I jumped into the fray.

I grabbed Che, threw him off Noah, and the music stand bounced off the white tile floor. Che then turned against me with all the force of his military-fit body, and we wrestled until I had him pinned on the floor in a headlock. Still, Che resisted my restraint, cursing me and struggling until he realized he could still punch me in the back of the head, which he did repeatedly, with all his might. I squeezed his neck harder—dangerously hard—to quell the attack. The fight ceased to be friendly at all. With all the screaming and punching and body slamming, the emotions we had been trying to drink away bubbled up.

Che managed to flip himself, and although I held onto his neck, he slammed me against the wall. I slammed him back, choking harder. I did not dare release him or surely he would punch me unconscious, the mood he was in. I had never seen Che like that—furious, enraged, out for blood. Finally, though, I sensed Che tiring and let go of his neck.

We sat on the floor, gasping for breath, while Noah and Freeman raged in equal fashion right beside us, knocking over lamps and smashing the photos on the wall. Instead of relaxing, though, it seemed like I had absorbed Che's rage. I felt it myself now and wanted to fight for no reason. I wanted to hit and cause harm.

We both sat on the cool floor, catching our breath from the rumble. That's when Che leaned close to me, pointed at his own face, and, in a voice meant to antagonize, said, "Come on, Thad. Hit me. One free shot." As he talked, he wagged his head back and forth, like a schoolyard bully taunting a little kid whose ball he just stole.

This was a weird thing Che had done to me throughout childhood—giving me a chance at a free shot. It was a way of taunting me because he knew if I took it, he would have a free pass to kick my ass. He was seven years older than me, so he had always been many orders of magnitude bigger than me. I had never taken the bait because I knew it was a trap. Even though Che was generally easygoing, he was like the rest of us in that rage could always bubble up at any moment. Our family knew anger well. We did not shove anything under the carpet. Shit had never gotten this crazy before, but when we were pissed off, we'd fight and did not much care who with.

"Come on, Thad," Che taunted again. "One free shot."

All year, at Cal Poly, I had been training at a kick boxing studio and learned to punch with the full force of my body. As I looked at my oldest brother, it crossed my mind for the first time that, although Che was more fit than me, I was bigger than him now. We were on our knees, squared off, so I leaned back without warning and rolled my weight forward with my fist to deliver the hardest punch I could, right into his face. It hurt my hand, and I liked the pain. Immediately, I wanted more, but Che fell, bumped his head against the floor, and did not fight back.

"Jesus," Che said, sopping blood from his nose with his sleeve, "I didn't think you'd do it."

"I would have done it with a baseball bat, if I had one," I said, suddenly vicious.

Che sat with that news in silence, as did I. He did not resent my having said it. In fact, he knew the feeling well. Ever since Mom got cancer, I think we had all wanted to goddamn smash and kill someone

or something on a regular basis. The fact that we had not been brawl-
ing like this every single day for the past ten years was actually pretty
miraculous. Che had two black eyes. My face was covered in blood, but
it was mostly his. We felt very close to each other in that moment, leaning against a piece of broken furniture, watching Noah and Freeman
go at each other like savages.

Freeman had Noah in a bulldog hold, leaving Noah with no de-
fense but his teeth, so he bit Freeman on the chest, arm, and ear. Freeman tried unsuccessfully to choke Noah out, screaming in pain all the
while. When I saw blood flowing from Freeman's ear like a fountain, I
felt obliged to help him. Noah hammered me good in the process, but
when it was all over, Noah's face looked like a purplish, too-ripe squash.
With the black eyes they both wore, Noah and Che finally looked like
the identical twins they had never been.

The fight abated, so there was nothing to do but drink more, and
soon Che turned morose. He wept and admitted he had so much anger
toward Noah he did not know how to ignore it, express it, or make it
cease. This had been a lifelong problem, but letting it out seemed to
do Che some good. For my part, I admitted I was miserable too. I felt
I had been forced to shoulder the burden of the farm. I could not bear
the thought that it might go under now but hated that so much of this
responsibility lay on me.

Che understood. He knew I had always been the family member
"most likely to run the farm someday." I was the one who welded machine parts and fixed things in the barn and built things in the wood-
shop. Loving hunting and horseback riding as much as I did, I was the
most embedded in Yolo County, and I had, after all, been Mom's axe
man from an early age. The farm was a positive part of me far more
than it had ever been for Che or Noah. All these things were true, but
this created an expectation—implied, never outright stated—that pres-
sured me to be the one who made sure the farm did not fail.

If things went south, Noah wouldn't have turned his life upside
down to save the farm, but I would have. Freeman loved the farm like
me, but he was so young, he did not even know himself yet. Che was

out, permanently. He never equivocated about that. That left me to keep Mom's legacy alive. None of my brothers wanted to put that on my shoulders, but there it was. I guess I put it there myself.

The farm was a part of me—like a parent and a child at once—and I couldn't go a day without thinking about it. As for Che, now that Mom was dead, he courted misery in his own way, feeling guilty for having left her to pursue his desire to fly. We were trapped inside ourselves, Che and I, and no amount of drinking, fighting, or crying could pull us out of these weird mental spirals.

At some point in the evening, we all passed out wherever we lay, like figures frozen in time. Immediately (it seemed) the alarm clock we had forgotten we set woke us up in time to catch the plane home. With semi-sober eyes, I noticed Che's house was irrevocably trashed. The dining table leaned on a broken leg; the futon couch had fallen through a glass coffee table; whatever used to hang on the walls was now ripped, smashed, or gouged. Che did not seem to give much of a damn. He commented briefly on what a mess we had left him and announced we had forty-five minutes to get our shit together.

We all giggled and joked as we threw our things in suitcases, talking about how ridiculous the evening had been. We made fun of each other's black eyes and bloody noses. Freeman was congratulated on holding his own against Noah, even by Noah himself. Che won the ugliest motherfucker alive contest with his double black eyes. Someone taunted me and called me a pretty boy for having no visible cuts or bruises on my face, although the back of my head hurt like an ice pick had been driven through it.

We somehow made it onto the plane, smiling insanely at the flight attendants, who looked at our bruised and bloodied faces, smelled the old booze we did not have time to wash from our bodies, and wondered what kind of freaky people they had let on their aircraft.

Truth was, the fight had done for our family what no amount of therapy could have ever achieved. We were brothers again. Whatever had been holding us back, blocking us, angering us, making us blame one another for the aftermath of Mom's death—it dissipated. The four of us were closer that morning than we have ever been.

Even today, decades later, we remember that evening fondly and even recall moments of the fight in exact detail. We love to talk about it:

"I can still see that music stand wrapped around Noah's neck. Che tried with all his might to choke him out!"

"Freeman had me good. I bit his ear because that was the only thing I could do!"

"Not going to lie, I was happy to see you fuckers all leave. But I started to miss you when everyone at work asked how I got the black eyes."

Today, we love to recall that evening and our ridiculous, all-out battle for blood as much as we like to remember how much our mother loved us and her farm. There is no denying that our unique upbringing with both its victories and failures are, quite simply, the things that make us, still and always, the only four animals of our species on earth. It was amazing that the fight ended up being a bonding moment, for what a brawl it was, but that is our family for you. Between all the drinking, fighting, and crying, we brothers knew there was no one else out there who quite got us like us. Nobody else had grown up with the combination of Dad's gift of ultimate freedom paired with the curse of his selfishness. Nobody else had experienced being able to take for granted the unconditional love and dedication Mom provided to both us and her farm. Few other Americans know the hard work of moving irrigation pipe or transplanting endless rows of vegetables, day after day, when you are just a little kid, but you have to help your family get the job done. No one else knows the creativity we had to utilize to keep ourselves entertained throughout childhood's long, hot Yolo County summers. No one else knows our lives, and we four will never know any other childhood but the one we had, for better or worse.

Come January 1, 2001, we needed to make a fresh start, whether we wanted to or not. Mom was gone, and all we boys had was each other. That New Year's Eve, a fist to the face seemed like as good a way as any to bring the family back together.

Afterword

My mother has been gone for over twenty years now. When I started to work on this book, I was not sure what would come from my effort. I had always wanted to put this set of memories into writing, and part of the inspiration to get it done was my brother Che saying that as soon as he got over Mom dying, he was going to "write that shit down." Che never got to do that.

It was painful but important for me to record some of my youthful, stupid, and egotistical memories. Part of growing up is doing dumb things, but making it to adulthood means that those dumb things have not killed you, ruined your reputation, or landed you in jail. Remember that, kids. This story reminded me, painfully, of the respect my ego wanted from others after Mom died, but at the time, it was respect I had not yet earned. Twenty years later, I can tell that twenty-year-old that his generation eventually earned that respect, but it took time and a pile of work.

It is easy and tempting to write history with a point of view that benefits a convenient narrative. I genuinely tried to not do that in this book, but I am human. Regarding accuracy, every word in here is true to the best of the ability of my first-hand memory, but many things have been left out. As I edited the final version of this book, some items were just too real or too damning to some people. In other cases, certain points of view were too raw, or too weighted in what I now feel was the incorrect emotion of the time. In the end, I asked myself two questions. The first: Would I be comfortable talking about this item with anyone, including the people involved in the story, in front of all my family? The second: If I died before I could have a conversation with my kids about this, would I be comfortable letting this written document be what they thought about who I am?

Those two questions and this writing process made me realize that I still carry a lot of baggage about those years after Mom died. At one point, I read deeply into my and Mom's journals trying to bring myself back to that year, and I had a full-blown emotional breakdown. In tears, with my guard up, I picked a fight with my amazing wife Moyra. I think about that now and believe it was my ego telling me that if my wife were no longer here, I'd be all right. That's messed up. Without fighting back, which she would have been fully justified in doing, she made a sage suggestion: "Okay Thad, time to give the journals a break."

Through the process I uncovered a fair amount of emotion regarding my father, too, who is alive and has read this. I didn't set out to make this as much about him as I feel it turned out to be. In fact, I made a focused effort to temper the narration of some of the stupid things he has done so that that his actions weren't what stood out about this book. Dad was both a major part of the first twenty years of my life and the initial spark of our farm. Of course, it was my dear mother who steadily tended that spark into a flame that still glows today. Dad and his behavior didn't just factor into the personal interactions within the family but polarized my mother, her family, and Terry—the people with whom I was closest. As a result, I was often left on my own, lost and unbalanced, while each of them dealt with their own complicated relationships with him. Regarding Dad, he has not changed, but I genuinely believe he loves us and always wanted us to succeed. I'm glad that the process of writing this book and sharing it with him has highlighted some of Dad's best qualities, specifically his genuine open-mindedness and unwavering support for his boys.

Every decade or so, people in our community become more comfortable with my brothers and me as independent adults, and our reputations shift from having been associated directly with our father to a place where we all stand as contemporaries. As this happens, every decade or so, another skeleton or two somehow finds its way out of Martin's closet. Sometimes the skeletons are thrown at us, sometimes we find them ourselves, but as they lay shattered on the floor in front of us, it's relieving to have the ability to walk by them and not let them define any part of who we are.

A few years ago, when this project was in its infancy, Freeman and his wife Carol hosted a birthday party for Dad at their house, which used to be Grandma and Grandpa On-The-Hill's house. At the party, Dad gave a toast in which he recounted a version of history that was very different from my recollection of the same events. In fact, it was cringeworthy. In a mixed crowd of his cronies and family, Dad was unable to deliver a point of view specifically tailored to his audience, so he spun the stories of his earlier years to position himself as a victim. He described himself as the poor guy who got forced out of the farm and Mom's life for no reason. He attempted to manipulate the crowd into feeling sorry for him and implied that had he not been "kicked out," this farm rightfully would have been his. If spirits and ghosts existed, my grandparents and mother would have shown up in that moment with strong rebuttals . . . but the house did not shake.

History is an interesting thing. It is written by those who survive, not the dead, and it turns out that some supposedly historical stories can have many not-so-factual items in them. But if you say something frequently enough, people eventually believe it to be true, including the person saying it. I do not believe Martin made up his point of view, but yes, I have seen him lie, and I know he is capable of it. I am sure that, in his mind, in his reality, that point of view is real. He has explained this point of view so many times to audiences that did not have the knowledge or will to challenge him, that he really believes he is a victim.

The unfortunate part is that Mom is dead and no longer able to defend herself or bring to light her point of view. That said, it is my opinion that *Betting on the Farm* is a true and fair representation of what happened with my parents and our childhood. Both of my surviving brothers read this and offered suggestions that were incorporated. I understand that this is a personal story about myself but also about Che, Noah, and Freeman, and I appreciate that Freeman and Noah have been incredibly supportive with letting me tell this story. I also understand that had they told this story, it would have been different, reflecting their realities through our childhoods and the year 2000, which were undoubtedly different from mine. With Dad alive, I naturally had more time to ask him questions and get more memories from him. With Mom dead, I was not able to do that. Over the decades, much of my memory of her has faded in the same way that a fresh bouquet of flowers dries to resemble something similar but not quite true to the original's beauty and vibrance.

Recounting these events also gave me cause to think about both my families, the Barnes and Barsotti clans. Time has proven that my dad's family has been, without a doubt, a much more supportive and engaging family to my brothers and me than this book's content suggests. They remain interested in what we are doing, reach out to visit when they're around, open their homes to us, and join us in our homes. As much as my mother loved them and felt hurt to not have them take her side, I get it. We can all look around at our families and ask ourselves what it would take to side against our own blood.

That said, my dad has recently turned his focus to claiming that all of academia is wrong about specific topics like HIV/AIDS and COVID-19. He hounds his family of academics every chance he gets. It makes me wonder if my dad's family is more sympathetic now regarding what my mother had to deal with thirty and forty years ago. It was the same type of raving, just about different topics. Personally, I miss the days when his conspiracy theory mind was focused on aliens. At least I found that conversation interesting.

The parts of *Betting on the Farm* that emerged as gems for me were those that recall our childhood stories. Those stories are still fun for me to read, and already this has jogged my memories of stories that did not make it. These stories back up the fact that we had a childhood that was unique and impossible to replicate. Those stories and our childhood are products for which both my parents deserve equal credit. Neither of my parents was perfect, but they pursued what they wanted to do and taught us to do the same. They broke completely out of the molds their families had created for them and made their own life together, at least for a while. They experimented, took risks, and were not afraid to do what had never been done before. They moved out to Yolo County's rural Capay Valley and into a way of life they had never before experienced. There, they were out of their element, overeducated, underexperienced, and surviving by little more than intuition, but their spirit and hard work toward a deeply held ideal helped build the organic movement. They truly were pioneers.

As an adult with life experience, I can acknowledge how lucky a human I am. Growing up, my brothers and I had a genuine belief that we were poor. This was not something we were told or asked to believe by our parents. It was based upon looking around and feeling that everyone else had better things: better clothes, better food, better equipment, better vacations, and some disposable income. There is no doubt that we all built up sizable chips on our shoulders about this.

Reflecting on that now, as an individual with more experience, I see that our parents chose to give us something different. They chose to forgo the middle-class American dream they were raised on and give us a childhood that could never be duplicated. We always had food, even if it was not the kind we wanted. We always had health insurance. Our public education was supplemented by our mother's expectation that we would do well in school. Our work ethic was built by her equal expectation that we would help out on the farm when it was needed. While our parents were not able to pay for us to go to college, they, Mom in particular, set the expectation that we would go, so we all did.

Beyond our parents, we brothers grew up engaged with both sides of our family, who were both successful in their own ways and proved to be role models from which we learned to behave. We were not poor. In fact, we were given opportunity beyond our imaginations and certainly had more to work with than those ordinary things other children had, which I used to long for thirty years ago. For this, I am grateful.

For the hardworking Americans for which poverty is a reality; for the Americans who have been born into impossible situations through no fault of their own; for the hardworking, talented individuals who found success harder than it should be because of their gender, race, or ethnicity—this story is in no way meant to disrespect the reality of being raised without the opportunities, privileges, and stabilities I was afforded. Simply put, writing this story helped me to look back at my childhood and acknowledge how ignorant I was to believe I was poor. This story has also helped me to realize how ignorant many people still are regarding the fact that our society delivers opportunity and success unequally between different groups of people.

Another gem for me in this story was memorializing my older brother Che, who ended up being the second great tragedy for our family in the same decade. On the evening of October 29, 2009, Che was the pilot in command for Coast Guard Rescue 1705, a C-130 containing a crew of seven including himself. They were dispatched from Air Station Sacramento to look for a boater that had gone missing off the coast of San Diego. Unknown to them, a flight of four Marine helicopters were on a night training mission flying without lights as they prepared for first-term President Obama's push into Afghanistan. The third helicopter, a Cobra attack helicopter fully loaded with arms, piloted by two United States Marines, collided with Che's C-130 in mid-air.

An epic explosion was heard and seen from San Diego. It ended the lives of nine servicemembers. Che was only thirty-five when he died. An ironic twist to the story is that Alfonso, the kid who taught me the difference between Black people and Latinos, who was the oldest son of our farm's first Mexican farmworker, Lala, had become a US Marine. Alfonso loaded and armed the helicopter for that flight. Che and Alfonso killed countless hours on the farm together as children while they waited for the workday to be done.

Che's memorial service was held at The San Francisco National Cemetery, and his celebration of life was held at the Golden Gate Club, adjacent to the cemetery. It was an amazing party. In fact, it was good and needed medicine for everyone's crippled souls. The people who were involved in Che's life came to give and get support, to share the stories and impacts Che had on them, ultimately helping Che live in all of us a little longer and a little brighter. It was an example of how a funeral can help with the healing process, the opposite of what we experienced with our mother's funeral. It was the celebration of Che's life that got the Barnes and Barsotti clans in the same location for first time since Mom's death. It was here that individual members of the Barnes and Barsotti families were able to have an exchange about losing Kathy. For some people, this was a funeral for both Kathy and Che.

It was not long after Che was killed that we, as a family, found our financial success. Ironically, only a couple of years after he died, we would have loved to hire Che for whatever salary he would have required to leave his stable government job as a Lieutenant Commander (LCDR) (04) in the United States Coast Guard and come work with us. Che had just finished his assignment flying helicopters at Air Station San Francisco and could have left the service. Knowing he wanted to keep flying, he agreed to stay in if he could fly fixed-wing aircraft out of Air Station Sacramento. In his "old age," he, too, was being drawn back to the farm, at least the farm's proximity, and owned a home in Davis. Had we been able to make Capay Inc. profitable only a year earlier, maybe we could have coaxed Che away from taking the transfer to Sacramento's C-130s. I do not lose much sleep over this anymore, but I still think about it from time to time.

During college, there was an event that foreshadowed Capay Organic and Farm Fresh To You "making it." This event gave some justification to our choice to bet our lives on the farm. The event was the EcoFarm, put on by the Ecological Farming Association, held annually at the Asilomar Conference Grounds in Pacific Grove, California. This gathering brought together the budding organic farming community to share knowledge about techniques, equipment, technical stuff, philosophical stuff, and just to generally schmooze. It was a conference that my parents, Dad in particular, helped get started in the early days but that I personally had never attended.

In February of 2001, I went to the EcoFarm for the first time, and, to my great surprise, I found aspects of a community I knew from childhood. Like Mom and Dad, the folks we met there had pioneered organic farming. Whether or not I remembered them, the members of this intimate community knew me and asked about my brothers by name. They remembered the stories of our births, including how my placenta hung out in a bowl in our family fridge for weeks. Several times at the conference, complete strangers commented upon a memory of holding me as a baby. They knew about Che's obsession with flying, my bad handwriting, Noah's high school pig-raising enterprise, and Freeman's comparatively large size as a baby.

As I attended the meetings and met the attendees at the conference, our parents' friends made comments that left clues about pieces of myself and my parents that I had not yet discovered.

"How's your dad doing with his new project?" asked one guy, referring to Dad's ruin in France, but the statement could have applied to Dad at most any time.

"That's great you guys are giving the farm a go. Nobody really thought that would happen," said some lady.

"Your dad, he was quite a visionary. I remember him from way back," added an old hippie.

"I remember once seeing your mom holding her head down," said a man I recognized, "and I told her 'Kathy, you keep your head up!'"

"I think you may have gotten the best of your mom and dad," someone else said. It took me a decade to understand that one.

"I found a lot of inspiration from your mother. There are not a lot of women in agriculture doing what she did," said another man. This stuck me as strange. It had never occurred to me that what Mom was doing was unique *because* she was a woman. I always thought it was unique enough for any human.

"You are organic royalty," commented a woman my age with a red UC Santa Cruz Banana Slug beanie. It was truly the first time I noticed anyone looking at my situation with envy.

Hearing about my parents from people who knew about me but whom I did not remember certainly provided an interesting perspective. More significantly, the conference demonstrated that we Barnes and Barsotti boys were part of an important community and that this little community had grown into a real industry with a future.

At that conference, I finally began to believe there could be a future for me in the farm that our mother left us. From my two-years-and-change worth of college education, I had come to understand that we could not half-ass this farm if we expected it to grow as a business. Mom had not just raised us on the farm, she had left it to us free and clear, which made it, essentially, a tested blueprint of a business we could all run together if we so chose.

So yes, we chose to run the business together. Most people who knew I was writing it assumed this book would be about that. It seemed to even bother people that the growth of the business was not the story. Yes, there certainly is a story worth writing down about the twenty years that followed Mom's death, but the truth is that neither Freeman, Noah, nor I can individually take credit for the economic success the company would ultimately build. However, I have no doubt that not one of us thinks the credit can be split equally either! With our lack of experience, the growth of the company was a task that no single one of us could have done alone. The key to our success was that we showed up every day, tried, and fought, because we cared about it and wanted to succeed. We also were always on the same page about wanting the farm to connect local and organic produce to as many people as possible, not just a niche group of foodies. Perhaps the most valuable thing we inherited was the piece of time that overlapped with the internet and organic produce becoming mainstream. With time, we got good at running the company, especially figuring out how to grow and run it without giving it away to the bankers or investors.

Our place in the organic industry is not one that we brothers get to take full credit for. My brothers and I never had the vision that my parents had. In my parents' relationship, my dad is still credited as the idea man, and my mother was the one who made ends meet. Together, they both showed us how to sell produce to loyal and like-minded customers. Terry, too, needs to be credited in the success of what my parents were able to accomplish. Terry was the change on the farm that enabled my mother to find her financial security, even if it was not long-lived. Terry was the one who bridged the gap for our farm between theoretical hippie stuff and real, boots-on-the-ground, get-the-job-done-right business. Terry was the one who taught me that I could get shit done just as good, and often better than, anyone else.

In the generational story of my family, my parents and Terry deserve credit for being visionaries and delivering a viable proof-of-concept, demonstrating that the organic foods movement was not a fad. Later, it was my generation that did the work and took the often-unreasonable risks required to bring the idea, and our farm's produce, to the mainstream.

Last, to my children, nieces, and nephews—you are ultimately why I wrote this story down. By the time you have read this, you will have first-hand knowledge of your generation's story. Your childhood will have been much different from mine, Che's, Freeman's, and Noah's.

Maybe your life will be a breeze, in which case I hope that you are humbled by the reality of what prior generations did to set you up for your life of ease. I also hope that you make a focused effort to understand how people with less opportunity than you live and that this humbles you.

Maybe you will need to deal with the immeasurable pain of a tragedy, in which case I hope you realize that it will hurt, but so long as you keep going, you will get through it. You will never be who you were, but five years later, you will arrive at the other side, where the pain has subsided, and happiness will exist again. During that pain, remember to make no permanent solution to this temporary problem. It may not feel like a temporary problem, but it is. Keep yourself alive. It will gradually get better. I promise.

Maybe you will find yourself in a situation where life is hard, in which case, I hope you put your nose down and do the work. However, first take the time to consider the most safe and reasonable path.

The odds are that, with time, you will experience all these realities. In all cases, in all scenarios, you will always be better off sticking together. When it comes to arguments and disagreements among family members, there will inevitably be insults and injustices where you will wholeheartedly believe you are right. In fact, you technically may be right, and the other person may be wrong. Nonetheless, finding a compromise that keeps you all on the same team is what will make your generation thrive. This will not be easy. It will take work. Finally and perhaps most importantly, you will never accomplish anything if you do not try.

I hope this, the story of my first twenty years on earth, is of some value for your journey.

Lots of love,
Thaddeus.

·ABOUT THE AUTHOR·

Thaddeus Barsotti is the middle of four boys who were raised on a small organic truck farm during the budding organic foods movement and bustling farmers' market scene of the 1980s and 90s. In July of 2000 their mother Kathleen Barsotti, who started the farm in 1976 with her then husband Martin Barnes, ended her battle with breast cancer. At that time Thaddeus and his brothers inherited her sixty-acre farm, Capay Fruits & Vegetables, and her five-hundred-member CSA, Farm Fresh To You.

In the following two decades, the second generation would grow the sole proprietorship into an enterprise that would deliver nearly three million farm boxes a year to customers across the West Coast and farm over a thousand acres of organic produce while employing over one thousand individuals. He currently owns and operates the family farm with his brothers Freeman and Noah and dearly misses his late brother Che.

Through this work Thaddeus developed a passion for the benefits created for society and the environment by a transparent food system delivering the most local selection of food from producers directly to individuals. During his journey he experienced how difficult it is to make farming and ranching profitable on a small and medium scale. Thaddeus is interested in driving the societal changes required to make profitability attainable for competent new or existing producers.

Thaddeus grew up attending the local public schools of the Esparto Unified School District in California's Yolo County through high school where he was awarded a full ride scholarship through the Frank H. Buck Scholarship program. Thaddeus earned a Bachelor of Science in Bio Resources and Agricultural Engineering from California Polytechnic State University, San Luis Obispo.

Thaddeus lives in Yolo County with his amazing wife Moyra and their three children–Lola Che, Lucca McRae, and Julien Francis. He is passionate about conservation and spends his free time with family and friends building habitats for wildlife and returning native grasses and shrubs to the rugged ranch he owns overlooking the Capay Valley.

www.thaddeusbarsotti.com

Printed in the USA
CPSIA information can be obtained
at www.ICGtesting.com
LVHW010346051023
760137LV00003B/59